Living On The Inner Edge

A Practical Esoteric Tale

BOOK ONE

For those who aspire to the Esoteric Mysteries

Living On The Inner Edge

A Practical Esoteric Tale

BOOK ONE

For those who aspire to the Esoteric Mysteries

Cyrus Ryan

AXIS MUNDI
BOOKS

Winchester, UK
Washington, USA

First published by Axis Mundi Books, 2018
Axis Mundi Books is an imprint of John Hunt Publishing Ltd., 3 East Street, Alresford, Hampshire
SO24 9EE, UK
office1@jhpbooks.net
www.johnhuntpublishing.com
www.axismundi-books.com

For distributor details and how to order please visit the 'Ordering' section on our website.

Text copyright: Cyrus Ryan 2017

ISBN: 978 1 78535 780 0
978 1 78535 781 7 (ebook)
Library of Congress Control Number: 2017945653

A CIP catalogue record for this book is available from the British Library.

Design: Stuart Davies

Cover painting: The Divine Teacher, Avalokiteshvara, the patron Buddha of the Trans-Himalayan Arhat School, by Author.
The Symbol on the cover represents the externalization of one of the inner ashrams/schools in the West.

Printed and bound by CPI Group (UK) Ltd, Croydon, CR0 4YY, UK

We operate a distinctive and ethical publishing philosophy in all areas of our business, from our global network of authors to production and worldwide distribution.

CONTENTS

Acknowledgements

This book would not have come to fruition without the constant support and encouragement of my wife, Susie Ryan, who helped both in editing and in organizing the overall effort. I especially would like to thank Ludmilla Yermakova for her painstaking effort in underlining concepts that needed clarification, editing and helpful ideas and Diana Tuccillo for her help and support.

Preface

'The keynote of the new yoga will be synthesis; its objective will be conscious development of the intuitive faculty. This development will fall into two categories: first, the development of the intuition and of true spiritual perception, and secondly, the trained utilization of the mind as an interpreting agent'. (*Treatise on White Magic*, Alice A. Bailey, Lucis Press 1934, p.429)

Although Living on the Inner Edge is an occult memoir, it in fact illustrates how RN, our teacher, blended various esoteric and spiritual teachings into one new form. In one sense we were Theosophists, in another sense we practiced Vajarayana Buddhism along with the self-observation techniques of the Gurdjieff/Ouspensky Work ideas. We followed no direct school of thought, no lamas no gurus. All of our work was on the inner realms of experience. Through constant training we developed true spiritual perception. We studied the esoteric ideas of Theosophy and included the works of the Tibetan Master through Alice A. Bailey as Theosophy. We were not glued to traditional Theosophy, to Blavatsky or Judge. We followed the trend of esoteric thought as it evolved in the West. For practical work we studied the Yoga Sutras of Patanjali. To get a deeper understanding we studied Sanskrit so we didn't have to rely entirely on translations. We found the knowledge and ideas of the Gurdjieff/Ouspensky Work cut through to the bare bones of the human machine. We visited many groups, teachers, and read as much as possible to see what we could learn and apply as our own group work evolved. We were not scholars. The vast details of the Buddhist canon didn't interest us. What we were interested in was breaking everything down into its 'essence', to the simplest form that could be applied to increase our knowledge and know how in practice.

I called my memoir, *Living on the Inner Edge* because it is a

1

synthesis of esoteric teaching; it is a new way of approaching the esoteric traditions of old, not changing them, only reconfiguring them to suit a disciplined, spiritual life while still living, working, enjoying, and raising families in our modern techno-driven age.

Introduction to the Group Work

Meditation, diligence, and perseverance,
These three are the horses of the Mind.
Self-awareness, self-illumination, and self-rapture,
These three are the fruits of the Mind.

(1)

The Master D.K., known also as the Tibetan, expresses in his teachings, throughout the books by Alice A. Bailey, the importance of 'Group Work' and teaches us that our Soul on its own plane, the higher mental, belongs to a 'group Soul'. He also mentions that it is rare for members of the same soul group to come together on the physical plane but when they do, it is very special. He also points out that groups will be soon forming on the physical plane and that there will be preparatory schools of initiation in the near future, as mentioned in *Letters on Occult Meditation*. Such schools will be externalizations of certain ashrams of the Masters. I was a member of one of these unique groups for a number of years, actually just over 30 years. This group was an experiment by the Masters to see what would happen to a group of Western aspirants subjected to various spiritual energies and events. We were contacted by one of the Masters in 1978. It was not at all as we would have imagined, not at all like the stories that you read about in the occult books. The Master didn't magically send letters through space as they did with H.P. Blavatsky, nor did the Master appear and dictate lessons as in the case of Alice A. Bailey (A.A.B.). The contact was very short without any explanation. The Master gave us a 'word of power', a mantra with a particular tune, rhythm and focus. Coming directly from the Master, this word of power was charged with Divine Shakti/energy linking us both to this Master and an ashram on the inner plane. This is an important key point. It is the link with the shakti/energy of this Master that made this word of power alive. It is like you're plugged in! When we first got it, little did we know what would happen! We were like guinea pigs in a maze trying to find our way, having been given a powerful tool and a partial map. The all-powerful, mysterious law of karma was at work.

This word of power was like a seed and in time, through trial and error, grew into a tree of knowledge. The Master who gave us this precious jewel overshadowed our group of seekers for several years but did not directly contact us very often. Yet he was there. As a group we received inspiration and inner guidance as other contacts with other Masters and Devas eventually ensued. These Masters did *not* carry on conversations with us, they were *not* channeled entities nor did they tell us that we were good disciples or that the world was going to get better. Instructions were short and to the point, generally through inspiration about meditation, or methods to overcome certain types of negative forces. Our intuitive insights were tested constantly as was our ability to listen inwards and discriminate between truth and falsehood, between personality and Soul. We found many practical hints that were hidden in the teachings given out in the books of Alice A. Bailey and Theosophical works, plus various writings on esoteric philosophy that helped to guide us. These hints had to be tied together and, in time, they became a body of esoteric dharma in line and in harmony with the Sanatana Dharma, Ageless Wisdom of India and Tibet.

This small group of disciples that lasted for over 30 years has never mentioned or advertised the fact that certain mysterious Masters of Wisdom had made contact with them. *Living on the Inner Edge* is my spiritual memoir of these events, of what happened through these years, along with some of the esoteric teachings we discovered.

The Guru, the disciple, and the secret teachings
Endurance, perseverance, and the faith;
Wisdom, compassion, and the human form;
All these are ever guides upon the Path.
(2)

Further, the purpose of this book is to describe what we learned and to add it to the body of esoteric knowledge that is already existent. Our Work follows the Sanatana Dharma, Ageless Wisdom, or the Esoteric Traditions that have existed for ages, only trimmed down and made applicable for the modern world. Along with the teachings of the Master D.K. as presented by Alice A. Bailey, we studied different schools of Hinduism and Buddhism, plus Kabala, Sufism, Western traditions and the teachings of Gurdjieff as given out and explained primarily through the writings of P.D. Ouspensky and Maurice Nicole. From these different schools of thought we saw how in fact they are very similar, and like a large picture jigsaw puzzle we fitted the pieces together, building our own body of thought and practices. Most esoteric books, sutras, and spiritual stories generally talk about very advanced initiates or Masters, realized yogis or concepts that are highly developed in scholarly works that are difficult to comprehend. In this book I will discuss and describe our story, outlining some of the struggles of the aspirant, successes and failures, and what we found out about the forces of resistance. In the second part of the book I will describe some meditation methods that we tried, tested, and then used in the group work. In the appendix is a transcript of one of our teacher's lectures, *The Science of Transformation.*

First Awakening

Some changes that occur in life are hard to explain, they just seem to happen because of external events which make a big impact on us. The Esoteric Work, when understood, gives the tools that help explain why things happen. My parent's household was very ordinary. They were a middle class family that held on to those conservative life principles of the late 50s and early 60s. My father was a salesman and my mother was a homemaker. They played a lot of golf and card games as they belonged to a private golf club. They became very good at poker and bridge. When I left home at twenty I already knew, though I didn't understand why at the time, that I didn't want to live the same life style as my parents. Within a year I was a vegetarian. The strange thing was that I didn't dislike meat, but the desire to eat it had vanished. I had no difficulty making the switch, and unlike some of my friends from those days, I never fell back into meat eating. I cannot say I was spiritual, but I was fascinated and spent time thinking about time and dimension. George Gamov's book, *123 Infinity*, was my favorite read at the time. This book showed me that time and dimension were relative to each other, and helped me to develop some ideas concerning the relationship between past and future. I also began to think about deeper questions:

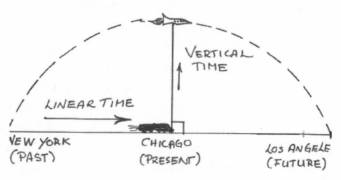

Linear Time and Vertical Time

whether the past was really dead and the future already formed?

I always enjoyed and shared with so many this diagram (above) where a comparison is made between linear time and vertical time. In linear time one travels, in this case on a train from New York to Los Angeles, and is presently in Chicago. New York represents the past, Chicago the present, and Los Angeles the future. When you're in Chicago, the present time, New York is just a past memory and LA a future anticipation. But if one is in a satellite a couple of hundred miles above Chicago, one can see New York, Chicago and LA at the same time. In this analogy, vertical time represents a heightened state of conscious awareness, detached from the flow of linear time, thus the now of vertical time includes past, present and future of linear time. Thus the past exists and the future also exists when one's state of consciousness transcends linear time, realizing another dimension or existence. One of the powers of the Buddha Amitabha is to cut through the smallest moment (ksana) of flowing linear time to enter into a deeper realization of reality. This idea just fascinated me and helped to explain how some people get future glimpses by momentarily touching some aspect of vertical time.

Later a buddy of mine gave me a book, which I still have, *Vedanta for the Western World* by Christopher Isherwood. Although it was a basic book, at the time, it was over my head but it intrigued me deeply. Not long after getting this book, following the wishes of my girlfriend, I started doing yoga, having no clue what yoga was. I persevered, even though my body was like a stiff two-by-four but eventually I began to loosen up. A couple of years later, through two other friends, I started doing Tai Chi, travelling twice a week to a small studio in the back of City Hall, on the edge of old China town. So now I was doing both Tai Chi and Yoga. Around this time, I came across another book, *Raja Yoga* by Swami Ramachuraka, which was a book on meditation techniques. One technique stood out in my mind, and I started to practice it sporadically. The practice was to visualize a flame, first outside you, then pull the visualization into the heart chakra. This was to stabilize the mind and counter the constant movement of thoughts. This focusing on the flame became the basis of learning about real concentration. This technique seemed to work and I found at times that the flame that I was visualizing seemed very real, and I noticed when this occurred there was this feeling or sensation of a 'silence', that seemed to surround and even touch me. This was not just an ordinary quietness, like in a quiet room.

One day at yoga class, after finishing our asanas, yoga postures, we sat in meditation posture and we chanted the OM in unison, and it seemed that we touched an inner harmony and we were all being lifted up momentarily into another aspect of reality. I felt this unity. It was an intriguing sensation. This struck me very deeply; however, at other times, when the yoga class tried sounding the OM it didn't have the same impact. Next I was introduced to the book, *Autobiography of a Yogi* by Paramahansa Yogananda by one of the students in the yoga class. This book, as it has for many aspirants around the world, opened my eyes to the hidden arcane secrets of the mystics and the possibilities of spiritual experience. I didn't understand much when I first read this book, but it was the thrust block that truly set me off on my spiritual quest. Like many spiritual books it should never be read once. Reading it once only gives one a taste of what's intended. Such books should be read and pondered on over several years in order to get the full flavor and digest the teaching that is given.

The yoga class I was attending arranged a weekend, two-day retreat in the country just north of the city. Amazingly about 50 people signed up to take part. Fortunately, the facilities were more than adequate and there were about 70 acres of land to walk around and enjoy the natural beauty of the place. It was early spring and most of the snow had melted and the weather was just warming up. Unknown to our yoga teacher, and most of us, an ochre robed, Indian swami, who was travelling from Los Angeles back to India, had stopped in Toronto for a couple of days and somehow had been invited to our retreat. I can't remember the actual connection but the swami only stayed for the first day of the retreat. The yoga teacher was gracious and asked the swami if he wanted to give a talk on Yoga. He complied and gave a short talk; saying that meditation was the key to yoga and that doing Hatha yoga asanas was just good for health and not of much spiritual benefit. Our yoga teacher did not like that; you could see visually how upset he was. The swami then asked if anyone wanted to meditate with him. Surprisingly, only I and five others decided to follow along and meditate with him.

The swami led us in a meditation of mandala visualization, but the main thing was I seemed to hear him in my head. The visualization became so real, bright and dynamic, as if it was alive. Then all of a sudden I heard him say, "I couldn't go any further, and the visualization stopped and just disappeared. For me, this meditation experience was amazing, I felt energized and lifted up so that my inner awareness was bright and I felt excited in a spiritual sense. This was no ordinary swami, yet after the mediation no one went to talk to him or to ask questions except me. The swami, whoever he was, when I went to talk to him seemed totally detached and distant. I knew so little; I didn't really know what to ask him. What was interesting is that the energy of this meditation seemed to stay with me for almost a month. At first, when I tried to do the meditation over again, it would almost start by itself, but as time went by it faded from me until I could not remember any of it. This experience strongly motivated me, and I started reading more and searching for meditation groups, and I still regularly attended the yoga classes. I was finally becoming more flexible.

Finding the Group

Then one day a friend of mine gave me a number of a group who had left a small advertisement at the Whole Earth health food store. I called the number and the individual who answered asked me if I had read any Alice A. Bailey books or if I was a member of the Theosophical Society (TS). I told them that I hadn't and wasn't and they hung up. The next day they called back and a different individual asked me almost the same questions and I repeated my answer but they said if I was interested in attending the meeting, come to the TS the following Thursday evening around 7 p.m.

I went, and found a small group sitting on chairs in a semi-circle in a basement room of the TS. At the head was a short, round, oriental gentleman in a sports jacket and tie and sitting beside him a much taller lady with a very colorful tie-dyed type of dress. Everyone was sitting quietly waiting for RN, the teacher, to begin. At first, I had some difficulty really understanding what he was saying, because of his thick accent. It took me some time to get used to it. He started the class with a short meditation to get 'into Essence' he said, and to be centered. I was totally surprised that the first part of his guided meditation was to focus on the golden flame in the lotus of the heart, picturing your body at the same time as empty and hollow. This is the meditation technique that I had already learned about from the book, as I mentioned before, *Raja Yoga*. He didn't allow anyone to take notes either. He mentioned that this meditation he was giving us was based on 'Vedanta', where you try to detach from your thoughts, emotions, and the physical body. This early meditation was called, 'not this, not that'. For instance, during the meditation you would create a mental picture of an event that caused you to be happy, then repeating this but visualizing an event that made you feel sad. You were to observe this as if you were watching TV. What this meant was to see it from a distance, not to get caught up in the memory. Not to get identified. Then you would try to feel yourself as the Essence, and realize that you are not your emotions. Then you would do the same with your thoughts. First it was necessary to see your thoughts as they constantly flow through your awareness. Again, you have to realize that you're not your thoughts. Then realize that you are the Essence, the Soul, and a point of Light. Once the meditation period was over, RN moved directly into his lecture after which there would be questions and answers and a discussion.

To the side of him he held, on a large type of clipboard, a multi-colored painting of various symbols. He lectured on something called 'Atma-Vidya', the Occult Constitution of Man and the Masters of Wisdom. I didn't understand much of what he was discussing, but something in me did, and I knew this was the knowledge I was longing to know. This was the beginning of the group. They were meeting every two weeks for a lecture and a short meditation. I came to the group just after *WESAK in May of 1975. (See chapter on Importance of WESAK)

Picture of RN during one of his lectures several years after my initial meeting below.

(Picture taken by author)

That summer I had already arranged a trip with a buddy of mine to California and missed the group meetings for the entire summer. While in California I maintained a daily discipline of meditation and even went on a ten day silent meditation-yoga retreat in the mountains. For me, staying silent for ten days was not difficult. It almost seemed natural, especially when you are in the mountains. I tried to do the meditation I learned in the group. At this point in my spiritual journey my meditation periods only lasted for 15 to 20 minutes. I felt that I was still a member of the group as I was doing the meditation given out by RN. When I returned home in September, I enquired about the group meetings and found out that the teacher did not want me to re-join, since I had disappeared for so long. I had told him that I would be away for the entire summer. Fortunately, one of the group members interceded for me and I was allowed back in. Thus began my association with this little group and then karma took over.

A group needs focus, our teacher provided that focus. He was just called RN. Our group was very small and over time it became more of a family. RN had three children who at different times were members of the group, too. All the members of the group were professionals, including RN, who was a flavor chemist and the rest of us all worked at various jobs from lawyer to teachers and in the service industry. We were not a group of dreamers but instead we were practical and down-to-earth individuals. "A group is brought together under karmic law, ashramic necessity and soul direction." (3)

As a flavour chemist for a large international corporation, RN had a very analytical 5th Ray (see section explaining Seven Rays) approach to teaching. He explained to us that the occult/esoteric teachings, like chemistry, were in fact an exact science. Everything was based on Law. RN had spent many years studying before he met us and built this group that lasted just over 30 years. RN did not cast himself as a guru. He was a teacher on the way.

The person who has found the way
Can pass on the gracious teachings to others;
Thus he aids himself and helps the others, too.
To *give* is then the only thought. (4)

When the group first started to come together in the early 70s, RN's knowledge was comprised of what he had gleaned from Theosophical books, plus his heritage. He was born in Indonesia with a Chinese father and Indonesian mother. He was exposed to Buddhism at an early age but by 16 had, through an older friend, discovered Theosophy. He told us that he had his first awakening while meditating during the Full Moon of WESAK, at the ancient Buddhist temple of Boro Budur on the island of Java.

RN eventually came to Canada via Holland. In Holland he discovered his talent as a chemist with a keen sense of smell, which led to his work in the flavor industry. He lived in a small town outside The Hague, with his wife and two children. He spent most of his free time studying spiritual books. His first marriage went sour as his wife, his high school sweetheart, got pregnant from his best friend. After his divorce he set sail for Canada, and very soon met a travelling Australian woman whom he married and started a new family with in Toronto. RN's two older children stayed in Holland, only coming to Canada many years later.

When I met RN, his wife was pregnant with their first child.

The experience of a small spiritual group and learning from a mandala was intriguing and totally new to me. Even the title, the "Occult Constitution of Man", gave me goose bumps as I sensed that a door to a new and maybe secret knowledge was about to open. RN had designed this occult mandala and his wife had painted it in very bright colors under his direction. He said that this Mandala was the key to understanding both oneself and the esoteric teaching of the Master D.K. This was the teaching on 'Atma Vidya', the radiant knowledge of Self or Personality, Soul, Spirit (see diagram below). These diagrams were very helpful in getting insights into the deeper teachings. Each diagram was an expression of a complex teaching in a two-dimensional form, based on geometric symbols and color. In a way, each of these diagrams synthesized an entire teaching that you would have to read an entire book to understand. This was like a shortcut. Over time, these diagrams evolved and RN added subtle changes that expressed more of the esoteric truths.

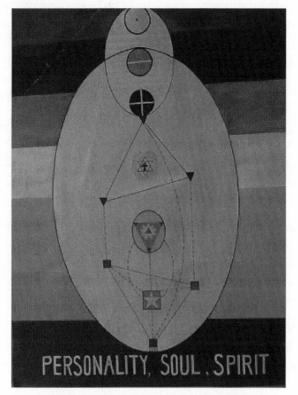

Personality, Soul, Spirit (mandala)

Mandala designed by RN.

The Master D.K. points out in a footnote in *Treatise on Cosmic Fire* that there are four branches of knowledge in India

1) Yagna Vidya, the knowledge of ritual.
2) Maha Vidya, magical knowledge.
3) Guyha Vidya, the mystic knowledge of sound, mantra.
4) Atma Vidya, the relation between the Greater Self and the little self.

The wisdom of Atma Vidya includes the other 3. (5)

Atma Vidya explains how the One Life and Light, the source of All, the OM manifests through the seven planes, from Adi, the first plane, down to the physical or 7th plane (Vaisvanara). As the ONE Ray (Spirit) from this Greater Life (ALL SELF) descends, it separates from this One Life and individualizes as a self-contained Soul (Jiva Atma). From this Soul, this individualized self-identity sends its ray of life and light (consciousness) to its reflection, the soul in incarnation, the lesser light, the Essential Nature. From here this life energy – now prana – radiates to the individual form that lives and thrives on the physical plane. It is this Essential Nature, the soul in incarnation, the lower light, that has to be awakened from its sleep. The 'lower light' is that which is hidden within the human being, the personality, on the physical plane. "This light, at a certain stage of man's experience, is awakened throughout the physical body and blends eventually with the 'greater light' (5). This is a most esoteric point the Master D.K. points out in Rule Two in *Treatise on White Magic* and I will discuss it further shortly.

Atma Vidya explains the function of reincarnation, karma, and the evolution of consciousness. These are three indispensable concepts that the aspirant to esoteric knowledge should understand thoroughly. RN explained to us that the teaching of Atma Vidya was very old and that meditating on the Mandala of Atma Vidya was like a mystic key that could unlock the doors to many esoteric systems, plus transform you in the process. It would help to awaken the 'higher manas', the higher abstract mind, through contemplating the ideas expressed by the different symbols and aspects in the mandala. By using the creative imagination of visualization, in time, the teaching of Atma Vidya will awaken within you.

He also explained that esoteric knowledge is very different than worldly knowledge or the knowledge we use in our daily life. Worldly knowledge, that which you learn in school or university and your daily job, can be easily memorized and utilized. Esoteric knowledge on the other hand, has to be integrated with your inner being, not with the personality but with your Essential Nature. Thus Atma Vidya is understood in the silence of meditation over several years.

Heart of RN's Teaching

Atma Vidya was, for this group, the central map that could lead the neophyte to self-understanding. It was this study of Atma Vidya that RN focused on and worked hard to make alive in the innermost self of all of his students. Through this teaching, he was able to show us that the personality and the Essential Nature are two separate psychological functions sharing one body. The personality encloses and hides the Essential Nature. The wants and needs of the personality can be, and usually are, quite different than those of the Essential Nature; thus the need for esoteric dharma training. As the life of the Essential Nature grows stronger, the life and strength and grip of the personality weakens, is transformed and purified. It is the Essential Nature that has to be awakened, not the personality. The Soul in incarnation, or the inner spiritual man, is the Essential Nature. This is one of the deeper esoteric truths hinted at by the Master D.K. in the teachings given in *Treatise on White Magic*. When you start to search for the Path, it means that the Essential Nature is stirring or awakening. It also indicates that the Soul, on its own plane, is trying to extend an invisible hand to guide the personality.

It is so common that many aspirants to the *Path of Return* assume that they have an advanced soul or 'old soul'. This is typical thinking of the underlying arrogance of so many aspirants and New Agers. They believe that, and even demand that, they should only be taught by a Master or a great guru. Such aspirants don't realize that the soul energy, which is just starting to bubble through to the personality, instead of working to build and stabilize the Essential Nature is actually leaking out and being absorbed by a particular aspect of the personality. This can lead to the awakening of spiritual ambition that feeds and builds a spiritual ego. The Master D.K. uses the story in *The*

Labors of Hercules, in the sign Aries to examine this fact. The key of this story is that Abderis, the just awakening Essence, still blended with the personality, has not yet developed any soul abilities and thus could not succeed in controlling the stormy emotional nature or 'kama-rupa' that is represented by the Man-Eating mares. It's important to use your intuition when reading about these labors instead of relying on the commentary. The Master D.K. dictated the stories not the commentaries.

Our group was living in a big city where living is expensive and always on the go. We weren't about to give up our careers to live in an isolated environment like some hermit. That is one reason the teachings of the 4th Way (see explanation of 4th Way) resonated with us early on in the group work. The essence of Gurdjieff's 4th Way teaching is that man *'cannot do'*, because *man is asleep* and must first awaken and in the process build a soul. This is an extremely profound occult concept and not easy to comprehend its real meaning at first. The Master D.K. explains the building of the soul in a more positive and descriptive way by explaining the means and purpose for the unfoldment of the three-tiered lotuses in the causal body and the teaching on the sub-planes. This process of the unfolding of the lotuses is, in fact, another way of saying that the aspirant is building a soul. The truth is that the Essential Nature is like a baby. Remember the story of the baby born in the manger! In that story, the baby represents the in-born Christ nature or Essential Nature, and the manger represents the heart chakra. So the Essential Nature when it awakens is like a newborn baby. Babies cannot just get up and walk, talk, and do things. This is the state of the Essential Nature of most aspirants. For people who have as yet to discover the dharma, their souls are asleep relative to the physical plane. The little baby will just lie there with their tiny arms and legs moving about, looking wide-eyed at the world. They have to be fed and taught and as they grow, then they can crawl, start to walk, and then talk. The Essential Nature is the same. Thus, like the little baby it cannot do anything in the inner spiritual worlds. Sometimes it can see or hear or feel but has difficulty explaining what it has experienced. It must be taught, educated step by step and given the correct food to digest. This food is the esoteric teaching and disciplines, plus the caring of a real teacher who guides the newly awakened Essential Nature. Then, in time, the Essential Nature grows and passes initiations, and then eventually it learns 'to do'. This can take years and even lives. It cannot be rushed.

Thus the dream of liberation is far away.

By the study of Atma Vidya the aspirant can see clearly the relationship between the lower self and the Higher Self, the difference between Spirit and Soul. So many spiritual people see spirit as no different than soul. They are under the impression that spirit is easy to contact. Through studying the Mandala it becomes evident that the experience of spirit is for those who have attained Soul union. Atma Vidya is a 5th Ray study, more like spiritual engineering, where everything has its place and purpose. Just like building a bridge. The difference here is that, as an aspirant to the Divine Mysteries, you are building a bridge between the tertiary world and the Spiritual world, between the lower self and the Higher self.

Group Expands

The group met at the Theosophical Society for some time, but then RN took a position at another company in a different city. The Toronto group would still meet every other week at a member's apartment to meditate and read, generally one of Alice Bailey's books, plus socialize and, of course, eat. Some of the older group members would travel to RN's new home in Montreal for a weekend of intense meditation and training. Eventually I was invited and able to make the trip and visit. RN's wife had given birth to a baby girl, who was born into the spiritual Work. In Montreal RN had met some new people and started another group. So when we visited, the two groups would be as one. Along with studying Atma Vidya, we started to explore the 'Tree Of Life', the mandala that expresses the essence of the Kabala.

RN had been studying the meaning of the Hebrew terms and symbols associated with the Tree of Life and then compared these terms with Sanskrit terms found in Atma Vidya. He found something in an old book that referred to the Buddhist Kabala. Something none of us had ever heard about.

The Tree of Life is a system of 22 Paths to Divinity that are guarded by great powers, the Elohim or Archangels. In a short time we saw that the Tree of Life was very similar to Atma Vidya and we could apply what we knew from one system to the other system. The knowledge aspect was almost exactly the same. The practice aspects, though, were quite different. The Tree of Life was also a system of invocation, to invoke secret powers. RN had an understanding of Ritual with the use of flower and incense offerings. We began experimenting with a group ritual and invocation using the Tree of Life. Unfortunately the forces that were invoked had a cold, unfriendly feeling. I remember feeling very uncomfortable, tense, not at all at peace or calm. We had chanted in Hebrew following the line of force in the invocation sometimes called the 'lightening strike'. After a very short time RN told the group that we were discontinuing our study of ritual invocation using the Kabala as he felt something wasn't kosher.

RN Goes to India

Even though we were experimenting with the ritual of the Kabala, our main studies at the time were still focused on Hindu Esoterism. Before long, we began experimenting with mantra, primarily the 'Gayatri', one of the most sacred Hindu mantras to Surya (its manifested form is the sun), the Logos. RN was certain that the deepest knowledge lay hidden in the garland of letters of the mantra of the Hindu Tantra. In 1976 RN, his wife and one year old baby girl, set off to India. Initially they stayed with some friends in Dehradun, a city in central North India. There, RN had an inspiration to travel alone to a sacred mountain in Southern India that someone had mentioned to him. This was Arunachala, the holy mountain of Lord Siva. It was at Arunachala where RN underwent an initiation. He was doing prostrations, over a thousand each day, as he continued chanting the Gayatri mantra when he received a Divine gift, a symbol which he called the 'Aruna Star' a six pointed star with a 'Shiva Lingam' in the center. From this experience a whole new world of knowledge, direction, and spiritual energy/shakti was received. RN realized that some time in the distant past, for numerous past lives, he was a devotee of Lord Shiva. The knowledge of the past was returning to him.

When he returned to Canada, he came back to Toronto, as he had returned to his old company just prior to his trip. At first he and his family stayed at a friend's apartment. He called a meeting just a few days after his return. We were all very eager to hear about their adventures in India. He explained the 4th Ray aspect of India as seen in the blatant disparities between the haves, the rich, and very poor, the have-nots, and also visible in the excessive bright colors of Indian art and dress. He also enjoyed how so many in India live such simple lives as they do not have access to the luxuries that are taken for granted in the

West. At this time, in 1976, India was a closed and very restricted economy, unlike today where all the mega-national chains have representation there. He also said that India was the true Holy Land, the inner planes were charged with sacred 'bhagans', spiritual songs and mantra. When he came to telling of his experiences at Arunachala the room became electric, we all felt some force had been released. There was a silent communication, an interblending of our auras that momentarily lifted us up and made RN's experience at the holy mountain of Arunachala very real. This was a group initiation of sorts as the spiritual energy/ shakti held within RN's Higher self was released and shared and felt among the group members. This is an example of a spiritual transmission that was experienced by the group. At the time there were still only about six of us.

RN needed a new place of residence and we set about finding him and his family a great two-floor apartment in an old house by a large park. For a short time the Montreal group would come down on weekends but eventually that group broke up and only the Toronto group remained. We decided to call the group 'Aruna Vidya' after the knowledge that streamed in from RN's experience at Arunachala. The Aruna Star, our new symbol, was very powerful. Too powerful it seemed! The Shiva Lingam at the center of the star added the 1st Ray aspect and we were not ready to play with 1st Ray energy. Unless your discipline is very focused and intense the 1st Ray can be very destructive. We were developing the Aruna teaching, adjusting it to reflect both the teaching of the 4th Way and Theosophy.

Discussing the 4th Way & Yoga

I am going to back track here a little bit. Although we primarily studied Eastern Esoterism, we also studied the works of G.I. Gurdjieff, primarily through the works of P.D. Ouspensky. There were certain aspects of G's teaching that explained many things. RN's special talent was to be able to get to the Essence or heart of a teaching and then translate it into a diagram. He pointed out that a diagram was a two-dimensional representation of 4th dimensional ideas. (See diagram below of the centers).

Through visualization and practice the diagram helped the student to ingest the esoteric ideas more completely than through reading. That's why the mandalas of Tibetan Tantra were so integral to the teaching of the Tibetan secret doctrine.

The term 'The 4th Way', I believe was coined by G.I. Gurdjieff but popularized by P.D. Ouspensky through his book *The Fourth Way* published in 1957. The 4th Way represents a modern approach to the Spiritual path, a newer approach to the Eastern methods of traditional spiritual attainment. The 'first path' or way, was that of the 'Fakir' who could attain a certain degree of spiritual success by putting tremendous stress on the physical

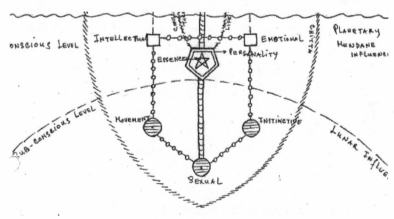

The 5 Centers

body. For example, there are many documented cases of these fakirs who would astound people by holding one of their arms, or some similar feat, in the air for months at a time without moving. This path depended on a tremendous power of physical will.

The 'second path' was that of the 'Monk', who engaged in awakening devotion or bhakti as it's known in India. The way of the 'monk' focused on evoking deep emotions of surrender to some deity or guru. The bhakti approach depended on receiving some form of 'grace' from *above* in order to achieve. The 'third path' was the way of the 'Yogi' which stressed a mental understanding of the workings of the totality of the mind. Through strong discipline the Yogi awakened a profound understanding of the workings of human psychology. In all three of these paths their adherents generally lived alone and away from society, isolated in caves, jungles or mountains, except for the monk, who would live in some monastery. The 4th Way, on the other hand, being a modern synthesis of the other three Ways, is meant for the modern man, living and working within an active society. The 4th Way utilizes the totality of a man's being, the physical, emotional, and intellectual aspects, and all the centers, united in an intense effort to awaken from the sleeping or mechanical way of living.

RN liked the teaching on the 4th Way because it is primarily a 5th Ray teaching, scientific and practical; with a secondary 3rd Ray aspect meaning it is based on universal laws. RN pointed out very early in our exploration of the 4th Way that it lacked the 2nd Ray; there was no love and compassion, it was more science. Therefore, he combined the wisdom tradition of Buddhism, 2nd Ray with the practices and teachings of the 4th Way. One of the reasons groups that only focused on of the 4th Way were a disappointment, RN pointed out, was because of this lack of 2nd Ray or compassion in the teaching. The danger, he taught us, was that many, and we met many, students of the 4th Way developed a sense of false pride that they had greater knowledge than other spiritual practices, thus creating an artificial spiritual personality on top of their normal personality. Gurdjieff hinted at this when discussing the idea of 'false group of I's'. This is very difficult to see when you're caught in this vortex of 'I's'. I will talk more on this subject later as the doctrine of the multiplicity of 'I's' is of great importance for the serious aspirant.

Along with all this, we also worked with certain sutras of the Yoga Sutras of Patanjali. We focused on the psychology aspect of the Yoga Sutras. The basis of these sutras is the concept of 'Chitta' or mind stuff. One of the hidden secrets of yoga is that even the mind is a *substance*, a very subtle substance. (This is mirrored in the teachings of the sub-planes as given out by the Master D.K.) This mind stuff, the sutras point out, reacts to both internal (samskaras) and external impressions (sparsa) from the environment. These reactions create modifications or 'Vrittis' of this mind stuff. The standard translation of the five Vrittis really leaves you wondering how to apply this teaching to one's self. One example, to illustrate this idea, is the standard translation of the Vritti, 'viparyaya' meaning 'wrong knowledge'. How do you apply this? What is wrong knowledge? This is a vast teaching on personal psychology but it requires direct self-observations through daily experience, and a teacher who can guide you in self-observation techniques. In one way, this is where the 4th Way teaching and Yoga meet. Both teachings stress self-observation as a means to self-knowledge. "When you walk, sit, or sleep, always look at your mind." (6)

The 4th Way has five centers that when bundled together make up an active personality. In the same way the personality is just the result of the constant activity of the five Vrittis as outlined in the Yoga Sutras.

For example, when an aspirant is depressed, feeling very down on themselves, and can barely do anything, being in a state of inertia, then the state of the Chitta in the Yoga Sutras is called 'muddha' and the resultant Vrittis is 'viparyaya'. What this means is that the mind stuff has become thick, like mud or a quicksand and the motion is sluggish, which results in some type of depressive mood. The worst thing to do when one is in this state is to take some pill to try and alleviate the negative feelings. Even meditation can be of little use when one is in this state. Instead, this aspirant should force themselves to exercise intensely or paint their living room. In the case of depression, the seekers' shakti or life force is trapped in a negative group of 'I's'.

Therefore, activity generated by intense activity can activate the next mental state of 'kshipta' and the Vritti of 'vikalpa' which changes the substance vibration of the Chitta from tamas guna, (passive) to rajas guna, (active). In the Yoga Sutras there are three states of matter: inert (tamas), active (rajas), and harmonious (sattvic). In other words, the mind becomes more active and dispels the slower moving Vritti and one will inevitably get out of the depressed state and start making progress again. This next state is one where the mind is very busy but not focused. From the yogic stand point it is still not a mental state conducive to mediation but it is better than being in a depressed state. Being able to change your Vritti through conscious focused discipline is the real *Yoga of the future*. For meditation one has to achieve the state of 'vikshipta', where the mind becomes ordered and the Vritti of 'pramana' is active. This is why study is so important. Studying with a purposeful attitude and attention on abstract subjects such as yoga puts the mind in order, but one has to be alert not to day dream (which is a vikalpa Vritti sneaking back in). This is the trick, to be alert, observant and not slip back into one of the lower or negative Vrittis. In this way, the Yoga Sutras become practical in a psychological way. In our group work we integrated many of the key ideas of the Yoga Sutras and the 4th Way to make it a very practical and daily applicable training. Even in Buddhist Tantra one of the key elements is being aware of your mind. Thus the Yoga Sutras, a 5th Ray teaching, gives the serious student a tremendous tool to know through observation exactly what state they are in, which can be applied in any esoteric discipline. It teaches you how to peer into your mind, then your awareness becomes like a search light. This is so important, especially when you start to deal with your own shortcomings or 'klesas', which on the deeper level becomes the 'Dweller on the Threshold' of occult teachings. When your self-observation reaches the point when you actually experience the 'klesas' as a 'knot' in the Chitta, or mind-stuff, then you know that you are starting to *see* in the occult sense.

We were serious students and the group, now that RN was back in Toronto, met regularly, at least three times a week. RN had a huge library and on weekends we would go to two spiritual books stores that were very active at that time. RN loved to buy books and so did many of us. We were all heavy readers. My own library started to grow by leaps and bounds. I didn't just buy books to fill book shelves, I read what I bought. We all had full sets of the 'blue books' by Alice A. Bailey, numerous Theosophical books, 4th Way books, Buddhist, Hindu and books on the Kabala. We also had several hard to find, out of print, occult books from the 1860s to 1940s. RN said the old occult books were much more reliable than the spiritual, esoteric books of today. There were far fewer books 100 years ago and generally the quality was of a much higher level.

We were busy developing our understanding of the esoteric teaching, integrating it with 4th Way ideas, plus the Yoga Sutras and Buddhism, too. I have to admit that many of the higher concepts passed over my head at the beginning. It takes a long time to assimilate so much knowledge. Study, as I mentioned before, was very important, but as an aspirant to the ancient mysteries, one has to develop their *being,* too. There has to be a balance, otherwise you get stuck in your head.

We all meditated at least twice a day. We did group meditations a couple of times a week, including Full Moon meditations every month. Life became very busy! The group work demanded a lot of our time. We all had our daily professions to attend to and sometimes going to work seemed like taking a break from the intensity of our group work. We studied, meditated, ate together, travelled, and eventually lived together.

My First Trip to India

In 1977 I went to India for two months during July and August. It was the wrong time to go. It was monsoon time! Hot, humid and it rained every day. RN said I should go since I had the time off work. He said that I should go to the Elora caves that H.P.Blavatsky wrote about. She mentioned that there were hidden caves that went deep underground and that there were still initiates meditating there. Also, RN said I should go to Arunachala and spend at least one week there. Other than that it was up to my own insights as to where I should travel to. This trip became a turning point in my Spiritual direction that was to affect me for many years to come and also the group.

When I got off the plane in Mumbai I was hit by a wall of intense heat, since one deplaned on the tarmac and walked to the terminal. Cultural shock was instant as the customs area was an organized chaos, but that was nothing compared to when I got out of the terminal. It was like a circus, with every cab porter person vying for your attention. Just so you know, in case you are thinking of visiting India now, it's not nearly as bad and the terminals are very western in design and organization. But back in 1977 it was a different world. I had to hold the door to keep it closed on the cab I took to my hotel in downtown Mumbai. I booked a fairly upscale hotel for my first night so the culture shock would be lessened, and I knew I would be tired and I would want a good bed.

The next day I took a cab to Pune, a small town several hours from Mumbai. At least this cab was better than my first cab and I made it to Pune in one piece. I went to see and listen to the popular guru known as Ragneesh. He had written several books and RN said I should go to his ashram to see what it was like and see if I could meet him. In Toronto one of our spiritual friends, D. Patel, was a boyhood friend of Ragneesh and they both studied and did some travelling together. He had told us that Ragneesh had become a teacher at a local college school but he dreamed of being a great teacher and worked with some businessmen to help promote himself as a guru. He was definitely successful at that. The ashram was very well organized, with a strong book marketing group. Ragneesh was a showman. He had a big white chair placed on a type of stage and the flock of followers waited patiently for his appearance. He reminded me more of a rock star than a spiritual teacher. I was very disappointed in the lecture and the next day I took a bus to the Elora Caves. This was another example of personality worship. Nice words but no real concrete teaching.

The Elora caves were just an overnight bus ride from Pune. Not far from the caves there was a small motel; they don't call them that in India, but it looked like a motel to me. I had no problem just showing up and getting a room; probably because it was monsoon season and most Indian tourists know better than to travel at this time. The caves themselves were magnificent but this story is not a travelogue. These caves were cut out of living rock, some as far back as 1200 AD. There were Buddhist, Hindu, and Jain caves. I meditated in one of the central Buddhist caves that had a large statue of what I thought was Vairocana but may have been Lord Maitreya. The statue had been somewhat defaced during the Mogul period in India. Supposedly these caves were at an ancient trading crossroads and were very active at one time long ago. RN suggested that I should try and meditate in one of the caves starting a midnight. These caves were old, dark, and eerie and the thought of spending a night trying to meditate there sent chills up my spine. I had brought a small inflatable pillow with me so I could sit on the ground, which proved to be perfect for meditating in these caves. Being the monsoon season, there were very few tourists visiting the caves during the day, which made my first experience there unruffled by the constant noise of busy tourists.

Initially, I meditated in the main Buddhist cave during the latter part of the day. That night, around 11p.m. I left my motel room and headed to the cave where I intended to meditate. It was a hot humid night and so dark, even with my flashlight the light could barely pierce the thick blackness that surrounded me. I noticed that the two night guards were sound asleep under the one and only lamp, on a bench over by the central Shiva temple which was a good distance from the Buddhist cave I had chosen to meditate in.

Elora Caves: Entrance to one of the Buddhist caves
(photo by author)

I entered the blackness of the Buddhist temple and set a small candle at the foot of the deity and also lit incense. Then, moving back about 15 feet, I sat on my inflatable pillow and sitting cross legged, I began to meditate. At first I felt very uncomfortable, alone, and still uncertain as to why I was doing this. As I mentioned, there was no one at all wandering around the caves at this time. Inside the cave it was so quiet you could almost feel it. The candle glowed, eerily casting dancing shadows on the cave walls. Then, after about 40 minutes into the meditation, suddenly there were three very loud bangs on one of the walls of the cave. More like, "Boom, boom, boom", that echoed even louder! My hair stood on end, literally! The sound vibrated and echoed through the entire cave, much like when you strike a giant cymbal. I immediately had thoughts to get up and flee back to the safety of my motel room. I could see myself running out of the cave like some cartoon character. It took a lot of effort to sit still, center, and continue with the meditation. But I persevered! Then I became aware that there was a huge bat moving towards me. It moved very slowly and its wings seemed to stretch from one cave wall to the other. I was frozen in fear as this giant demon bat moved closer and closer. Its movement was more like what you see when watching slow motion action in a movie. I started chanting and chanting at a furious speed, chanting silently, focusing my attention on the chanting and visualization of a deity. Yet I could still see this apparition of the enormous bat slowly and ominously moving towards me. I held my ground. Then just as it was about to reach me, it exploded and in its place there appeared a radiant figure, actually just the head and shoulders, just above me, smiling at me. It was not really a blissful feeling as a force seemed to rain down from this great being, through the top of my head, down through my entire body. The vision itself was in Technicolor and emanated a vibration of peace and a transcendental loving feeling. So I could feel both the transmission of shakti and the feeling of peace and grace. This intense, yet blissful experience only lasted a short time but it taught me about one of the laws of breaking through into a higher dimension. Once this total yogic event was over I didn't feel it was necessary to remain in the cave for too much longer and I headed back to the motel. I recognized the yogi who appeared above me immediately and I was totally surprised as I had never felt a strong connection with this historical yogi. He appeared in his 'samboghakaya' body, which is his subtle, immortal, spiritualized form that he maintains on the inner ethereal plane. I do not feel that I should mention his name here as that aspect of the experience is too private. When I left the Elora caves, I eventually headed north toward the mountainous region of Kashmir.

The next experience that happened to me, a short time after I had left the Elora Caves, created quite a lot of confusion in me. I was in a Himalayan town called Pahalgam, in Northern India, in the area known as Jammu/Kashmir. Pahalgam was a small town in the Himalayan foothills, sort of a jumping off point for treks into the higher mountains of the Himalayas. The following day after arriving there, I was walking upon a mountain path high above the village, visualizing the Shiva Lingam and chanting Om Nammah Shivaya silently as I walked. Previously, in the Buddhist caves, I chanted a Buddhist mantra and now, since I was going to a Hindu shrine dedicated to Lord Shiva, I switched the mantra. It seemed the logical thing to do! My visualization was remarkably clear and my concentration very focused. Then from

the lingam, the focus of my meditation that I was visualizing in my heart chakra, Avalokiteshvara (Ekadasamukti) exploded through the lingam in a fiery expression of Divinity. The radiant form of eleven heads and eight arms appeared, blazing with an aura of golden-white flames. I was amazed, even awe struck, but instantly I felt overcome with doubt. Who should I meditate and chant too? Who was my Ishtadevata? Lord Shiva or Avalokiteshvara? Why was this happening? This created a monster of a dilemma racing around my mind.

Author with a local guide, just before starting the climb and trek to the shrine cave of Amarnath, sacred to Lord Shiva (1977)

I had arranged a guide and rented camping equipment and the next day I started the trek to the sacred temple cave of Amarnath, high in the Himalayas. In this cave there is an ice stalactite in the shape of a Lingam that supposedly would glow during the Full Moon in the month of August. As I walked along I wasn't sure which mantra I should practice. Though the scenery at over 12,000 feet above sea level in the Himalayas was magnificent, I was still being plagued by this key thought about which mantra was my true direction. I did reach my goal of seeing this spiritual wonder of the white Lingam stalactite, but it was not the Full Moon in August, so it wasn't glowing.

Entrance to the cave at Amarnath, showing the ice Shiva Lingam.
(Photo by author.)

The fact is that so many pilgrims come to see these phenomena during the August Full Moon period, the trails become packed and each year there are deaths on those high narrow pathways. So it was better to go in July, as there were only a few pilgrims. This quandary of which path to follow stayed with me, maybe I should say haunted me, until I got to meditate on the banks of the Ganges River just outside of Calcutta (Kolcatta).

From the north I headed south, eventually reaching Calcutta after a brief stop in Varanasi. My teacher had told me to visit and try and stay for a night or two at the shrine of Sri Ramakrishna, called Belur Math, just outside of Calcutta. The life story of Sri Ramakrishna was one of my favorite spiritual stories, as it tells of his struggles on the Path of Liberation. Sri Ramakrishna was a pure devotee (bhakti) to the Divine Mother Kali. He was her vessel and he listened to her as a little child listens to its own mother. His story is heart-warming and also very informative.

I was still torn between following the Hindu Path or the Buddhist Path. I felt at home in India, where I knew and could feel that I had lived many past lives. After a long journey I arrived in Calcutta and made my way to the shrine of Sri Ramakrishna. Belur Math was built after his final Maha-Samadhi, the death of Sri Ramakrishna. His disciples, Vivekananda and Swami Brahmananda, used to meditate there in a small, private room that remains closed to the public but you can sit outside of it and meditate. I went to the main office to find out about staying in one of the many rooms there. Immediately they told me it was impossible because they didn't know me. I told them I was vegetarian and meditated and had read a lot about Sri Ramakrishna. They didn't care and repeated their refusal to let me stay. This upset me greatly, I felt discriminated against because I was 'white'. So I just sat down on the floor of the office and began to meditate. You can imagine their reaction! Most of the office staff were monks and they started to tell me to stop meditating and leave. I didn't budge. Eventually, a manager monk showed up and asked me to come into his office. He very politely asked me what I wanted. I told him I wanted to stay there for a night as my teacher had suggested; he had stayed there himself and found the place to be inspirational. Again, the answer was no. So I closed my eyes and started meditating again. He left the room for a while but came back, telling me that he had arranged for me to talk to the head monk. We left his office and he led me across to the far side of the compound. He pointed to a bench on a porch of one of the resident buildings and told me to sit there and wait. It was a very peaceful spot, just overlooking the Ganges River. Sitting myself down, I continued my meditation. After a while, a young monk, who seemed to be a novice monk, brought me some lunch on a traditional Indian metal plate. It was a delicious Indian vegetarian meal. I hadn't eaten much breakfast so I was really hungry and devoured my lunch with gusto. Then I continued my meditation. At one point during the afternoon meditation session, my individualized conscious awareness felt lifted up into a serene 'blueness' of peace and a deep stillness. For a short time I was just a point of awareness without body consciousness and no outward sensations. In this heightened state of awareness, I experienced a voiceless voice that told me that I'm Buddhist, aligned to Avalokiteshvara and I should follow that path. After this experience I felt like I was walking on air. My burning question of which path to follow had been answered. The serene peace and stillness lingered for a while. Then, back in my normal consciousness, I wondered what happened to the meeting with the head monk. So I continued meditating on the bench. Soon I was lost in contemplation but was interrupted as someone knocked on the bench. Opening my eyes I was surprised to see a policeman, actually the chief of police for the district. He asked about my purpose in coming to Belur Math and what I wanted. I told him but he immediately said it was impossible for me to stay there. He was very polite and asked me what I wanted to do. I told him that my next stop was to take a train to Chenai (Madras). He pulled out a walkie-talkie and in a minute made arrangements for a first class ticket on the next train to Chenai. I felt that my purpose for coming to Belur Math had been achieved, so I decided to go with this policeman. He took me to the station in his Jeep and put me on the train. The funny thing is that he also put one of his subordinates on the train, too. He wanted to make sure I left the city. First time I've ever been kicked out of a city!

I was very happy, yet a point of confusion started to set in, as the next stop on my trip once I got to Chenai was the holy mountain of Arunachala, which is the home of Shiva. Once I arrived there, I decided to chant to Lord Shiva and also do the Gayatri mantra. I would return to the Buddhist mantra once I left Arunachala. The main discipline that most aspirants did there was 'pradakshana' which means to circumambulate Arunachala as an offering. There were two main holy places to meditate on the mountain, Skandashram and Virupaksha Deva cave. When deciding to go there, it is a good idea to do some reading about the spiritual history of the area. There is a remarkable, huge Hindu temple with four towering pyramids, the Arunachaleswara temple in the town adjoining the sacred mountain. This is a classical Hindu temple, with pyramid entrances and the four courts leading to the 'holies of holies' in the center of the temple. I toured the temple but enjoyed being on the mountain more.

I stayed at the Rama Ashram in a small, plain bungalow, rising early each morning to do my walking meditation around the mountain. The main reason to do this discipline early in the morning is that it gets too hot out even by late morning. It usually took me about two hours to do the full circumambulation. If you are a real die hard devotee, you are supposed to do this walking discipline bare foot. I wore sandals. I have to admit that my meditations there were not anything special. The only event to note occurred as I was standing under the small stream of a waterfall to cool off by Skandashram; I had the strongest peaceful feeling of being home and that this had been my home in some past life. The feeling was so strong; there was no doubt in my mind that I had been there before. I did enjoy my time there as I met many people, other aspirants, among them Sadhu Om who was an acquaintance of RN's, and a girl from Boston who was into Indian classical dance. It was time to get back to

New Delhi to catch my plane home, to return to the working world and to explore my new found direction and to see what would happen with the group.

My flight back to Toronto left from Indira Gandhi airport, just outside of Delhi. I gave myself two days to sightsee and do some shopping. On my last day I was walking by an open market place, and as I was passing by one of the stalls, it seemed that it called me in. So I turned around and ventured into the stall which had many Tibetan statues of different deities. Then I saw, up on the back shelf, a beautiful statue of Avalokiteshvara with eleven heads, eight arms, and another twenty-eight arms. I had to buy it as it had called to me. My destiny was set! Now it was time to fly back to Canada, my first trip to India was over.

Shiva or Avalokiteshvara

As I flew back home, I couldn't stop thinking how RN was going to react when I told him that I'd become a Buddhist. Was I still going to be part of the group? Our center was a big, old house that I had rented and I lived on the third floor. In the meditation room on the second floor, on the altar there, was a silver Shiva Lingam which RN had custom made by a jeweler.

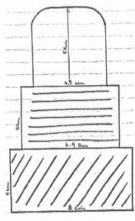

Now I was coming home with a statue of Avalokiteshvara and a whole new direction. But first, a strange event occurred just after I got home. At the time, I had a large drafting board in my place where I would work on my art projects. Early one evening, just after dinner, I was sitting at my drafting board contemplating what might be my next painting, when I just picked up a pencil and instantly drew a small symbol (see below).

RN's drawing of the Shiva Lingam. This is RN's diagram of the Shiva Lingam that he took to the jewellers.

Esoter Symbol

The first rudimentary drawings were done in black and I added color much later on. I didn't think much of the symbol at first and actually started using it as my signature at the bottom of my paintings. I knew it had a much greater meaning, but initially I drew a blank when I tried to figure it out or even meditate on it. A couple of years after being given this I experienced that there is some occult power and a much greater significance to it. To give a hint, the best way to start to break the code of this symbol is to apply the numbers one to ten to the symbol's make-up, using an understanding of the occult meaning of numbers. From a numerological point of view it illustrates how ALL manifestation comes from '0' or Sunyata. From the '0' or unmanifest comes the 3 (triangle) + 7 (component parts of the triangle) equals 10 the total creation. The ONE (Logos, Ishvara) manifested from the nameless unknowable Principle that H.P. Blavatsky. talked about, or Parabrahmin. The 3 in 1 (the creative force of manifestation) added to the 7 (the order of creation) adds up to the perfected 10 of the manifested form. Definitely something to meditate on, as there is a lot more to grasp about this symbol. This is an example of where you have to be able to use the abstract mind or as the occultist like to call it, the higher 'manas' to understand the symbol.

It took some time, but the group actually turned from chanting to Lord Shiva to putting Avalokiteshvara on the altar. It's quite a long story of how the change came about. There were many discussions of the pros and cons of these two different paths. RN loved the 1st Ray quality of chanting to Lord Shiva. He said that it cuts to the heart of deeper esoteric knowledge, like an acetylene torch cuts through metal. The Path of Shiva requires an individual who is very focused, with a strong will and perseverance, who is willing to sacrifice everything in order to reach their goal.

The path of Avalokiteshvara, on the other hand, was more 2nd Ray, therefore not as intense in its discipline. At first, RN felt that the mantra seemed weak as it was more of a circular movement instead of cutting like a knife or torch, which cuts through the many hindrances on the path. He thought the 2nd Ray path would be less demanding for the majority of aspirants, thus making it easier to build up a larger group. Also Buddhism is becoming more popular because of its 2nd Ray principle, focusing on love and compassion. Then he thought that maybe the group should be focused on the path of Avalokitehsvara, while RN himself would remain devoted to Lord Shiva. So we put the statue of Avalokiteshvara that I had brought from India on an altar in the main downstairs meeting room. RN continued to chant to Lord Shiva and to dig deeper into the teachings of Lord Shiva. The discussions still continued comparing these two paths. Then, shortly after this, RN had an intense dream experience where he saw that the path of Shiva was not for a group, that it's a solitary path and its destructive force was too much even for him. It was very difficult for RN to let go of his dedication to Lord Shiva, but he did it in the end and that caused a huge turning point in the group.

The group had started to grow as we had open lectures, and through karma some new people started to come. We applied the 7th Ray and 4th Ray by decorating the center, especially the large meeting room on the ground floor. Indigo curtains and a Buddhist orange back drop behind the altar was very eye catching due to the color contrast. The indigo being 2nd Ray and the Buddhist orange 5th Ray colors, plus pictures on the wall of different deities and mandalas added the 4th Ray through a variety of art. There was no furniture in the room, which was nicely carpeted with indigo and orange pillows scattered through the room and a few green plants too. It was an impressive meeting room. I had visited many other groups in both Canada and the USA and I had never come across a meeting room that was decorated based on occult principles quite like this.

Along with RN, I and one of our members, Edward, also gave talks. We tried various means of advertising, from posters in the local wholefood stores to small ads in the new age periodicals that were popular at that time. Even with the advertising it seemed that most of the new people came via some karmic connection, from people we knew or met through travels and other groups. This period was a fascinating time, plus we had fun, too. The house had a huge kitchen where RN would cook for all of us and we'd sit around at a custom made over-sized table, eating and talking about many diverse spiritual and occult topics for hours, usually late into the night.

Some Insights

We were always learning, discussing books that we were reading or the "Work" ideas as we called them. An early topic we discussed had to do with the difference between the *words* and *idea* and a *concept*. One of the problems in today's spirituality is that many aspirants have access to so many books that it is easy to be flooded with too much information. Thus, information is often confused with knowledge, because of the power of our intellects. Many aspirants just read a book or two and easily spout out the information they have read, sounding like an expert and giving the impression that they actually know it. This is the danger of the intellectual center. The Master D.K. mentions that concrete knowledge can act as a hindrance on the path too; just as the 4th Way also points out that an over developed intellectual center can be a big hindrance. One becomes top heavy, so to speak. This is one of the reasons why the great mystics and saints of history were not scholars and in fact guided their own disciples in such a way as to avoid scholarly debate and learning.

Too much esoteric information can even be detrimental to the probationer until they have achieved a more advanced level, where they can actually experience and apply these ideas in their practices and daily life. Until then, esoteric knowledge is only information. This esoteric knowledge has to be transferred from the concrete mind (mono vijnana) to the Essence mind (manasa vignana). The purpose of the esoteric doctrine is to help build a more inclusive picture of the workings of our planetary scheme and expand the minds breadth of thought, to deepen thought, so as not to become just a collection of theories and facts. Getting stuck on facts and only knowing the words brings to mind the quote from *Voice of the Silence*, "...the Mind is the Slayer of the Real." (7) In this situation a good memory can become a hindrance on the path to real knowledge. This is when you catch only the 'shadow' of the teaching, yet thinking it's real gives one a false sense of knowing and goes to build a false knowledge or an occult personality. As a famous Zen saying puts it, 'one looks at the finger pointing to the moon instead of the moon'. Once you've read a particular work, then you have to grasp the idea behind the written word. It takes time to think over what has been read, to mull it over, so to speak, gaining an understanding of the purpose of this knowledge. Eventually one has to be able to build a concept of the material in one's own mind, so that you can talk about the subject in your own words, talking from experience and one's own understanding, not repeating parrot like what you've read or heard from others. This is called, 'making the teaching your own'. This takes years and only comes through actual experience and through many hard failures, and step by step successes. You grow into the teaching. Then you become the Path.

We were now chanting "Om Mani Padme Hum" in our group meditation. The Master D.K. mentions in a footnote in *Treaties on Cosmic Fire* that, "the most sacred of all Eastern mantrams given out as yet to the public is the one embodied in the words: "Om Mani Padme Hum." (8) Our meditation started by visualizing our bodies as 'empty and hollow like a vase', to help detach or separate our awareness from the grip of the physical form (rupa). Next, we'd picture a golden flame in the lotus of the heart, focusing on this visualization. Intense focusing on the flame, picturing the body as empty and hollow, also helped to detach from the constant flow of thoughts that are in constant motion in the space of the mind (chittaskasa). When you could do this holding the flame steady, then you could start to feel your inner nature or Essence. Once you could feel that you were centered in your Essential Nature, then you were ready to chant. This centering process results in what the Master D.K. calls 'alignment'. Chanting from the personality has very little effect, whereas chanting while being centered in the Essential Nature creates a conscious inner connection to that stream of the higher forces.

This Essence nature is the feeling of one's individuality which is separate from the personality as a point of awareness or *'conscious self-aware identity'*, as the Master D.K. calls it. The Essence nature is like the hub in a wheel where the spokes are personal characteristics, and the outer wheel is the active personality as it functions rolling through daily life. To be able to discriminate between the Essence and Personality is the first big step forward for one's spiritual evolution. The trick is to be able to do it! To feel and eventually center in the *Essence I am* takes an enormous effort and constant endeavor to discriminate between the activities of the personality and the feeling of the Essence. The trouble is that everything in Nature is set up to prevent this. That's why it's a truly Herculean effort, based on discipline and perseverance, to awaken and that's why only a few can awaken at a time.

At this time I was teaching art, film, and one English course at a local high school. One day, during a grade 9 English class, some of the students who were working at the blackboard started making a commotion to get my attention. They wanted to alert me that one other student, Shirley, had written an unusual word on the board. She had written the word 'Atma'. Shirley was very shy and wanted to show me this word but was too shy to do it, so the other students made the fuss to get my attention. I asked her where she had got this word from. She said that it came to her in a dream and she wanted to know its meaning. I explained the meaning to her and the class, telling them the Atma was a Sanskrit word that had a profound meaning but 'true Self' was the best one to use in a general sense.

Philosophically, Atma is a complex term in Indian spiritual philosophy. Atma means 'Self' or more correctly, the 'Greater Self or One Self of the Universe'. Going back to the diagram of Atma Vidya, Atma is that *One Self* of the *One Life and Light* that permeates all manifestation. This we call Spirit. From the diagram, that ray from the OM which passes down through the seven planes to become that 'spark' or 'Essence' is still, in reality, Atma. As Atma descends into manifestation, deeper into matter, its different stages are given different names and eventually it becomes 'Jiva Atma', the independent individuality, or that sense of a separated *I-ness* that we all feel. We call it Soul. There are billions of Jiva Atma in creation but only one All Self that encompasses all the smaller selves, that is Atma.

Shirley started coming to some of our group meetings on weekends. She had a strong inner will and was able to meditate with us and soon gain a very good understanding of the esoteric dharma. She seemed a natural. I would also teach her after class, when she'd come to my art room at the end of the school day. She would come with so many questions. I enjoyed this one on one and could feel her Essence absorbing so much from our discussions.

Five Dhyani Buddhas

One of the other subjects we focused on was the teaching on the Five Dhyani Buddhas, also known as the *Five Buddhas of Transformation*. The books on this subject are primarily scholarly works and tend to be a very tedious read. From the few translations on this subject we could glean some basic ideas which added to our understanding. Using the Tibetan tanka or mandala paintings of these Five Buddhas, we were able to put together a viable practical meditation practice. Eventually, over a few years, a wealth of knowledge started to shine through. Most of us found that meditating on the Five Dhyani Buddhas was very difficult, as it required a very intense visualization discipline, plus a concentrated effort of pondering on the qualities of each of these Buddhas. We preferred to chant a mantra, plus visualization as it was more dynamic and seemed more intense. But chanting too much, especially at this early stage of our development, also had its drawbacks. Group chanting is much more intense than if you just chant alone. Therefore, when chanting in a group the forces which impact one's subtle bodies and centers are much greater. These forces and energies should be absorbed primarily by the *Essential Nature* and maintained there. But in many cases, especially at the beginning, they would easily leak into the personality. Until the aspirant was capable of staying centered in essence, the shakti/energy would leak out. Consequently some aspect of the personality would get over stimulated and this effect caused some of the group members a lot of difficulty. Thus, meditating on the Five Dhyani Buddhas was an excellent counter discipline to the chanting. When we meditated as a group, we would sit in a semi-circle in the main meditation room, facing the altar. Once the meditation was over we'd compare our experiences and then discuss the teaching.

One interesting aspect about the Meditation on the Five

Dhyani Buddhas is the number five itself. This number represents so many ideas in the esoteric teaching. These five Buddhas represent five great Beings, who represent five enlightened archetypes with their corresponding five 'manusha' or earthly Buddhas. For instance, Amitabha is the cosmic archetype for Gautama – the historical Buddha who walked on this earth 2500 years ago. On a lower scale, but a reflection of each Dhyani Buddha, there are the five 'skandas' or aggregates of matter that go to construct the qualities of our basic personal characteristics, our progressive, evolving life patterns, such as feelings, form, discriminating mind, ego-ness, and talents. The heavenly Buddha Amitabha represents the 'skanda' of 'samjna'. His wisdom is 'discriminating intelligence which cuts through all illusion' (pratyika vikasana jnana siddhi), thus Lord Gautama was the 'Light of Asia' spreading a teaching which would help humanity to understand and overcome the illusions of 'samsara', the hypnotic power of worldly life.

Another example is Lord Maitreya, whom the Buddhist considers as the 'future' Buddha, and is the Manusha Buddha of the Dhyani Buddha Amogasiddhi. The wisdom of Amogasiddhi is 'perfect magical action at the right time'. The quality of Lord Maitreya is, using Master D.K's terminology, 'service to humanity'. Many expect and hope that Lord Maitreya will manifest as an individual person to walk among us. Over the past few years there have been various spiritual groups promoting this immanent action. But Lord Maitreya generally does not manifest through rebirth as was the case in Palestine 2000 years ago, where he used the body of the advanced 6th Ray Initiate known as Jesus for a short period of time in order to fulfill his destiny on the world stage. The teaching on Lord Maitreya, as given out by the Tibetan Master D.K. is worth deep consideration as it gives much greater insight to the work of Avatars and the Masters of Wisdom. Since the Buddha, Lord Gautama, has left our system, tathagata (thus gone) only returning yearly on WESAK, it is

Lord Maitreya who is, in fact, the active Buddha *now*.

The Master D.K. mentions that Lord Maitreya is closer to humanity, but presently works by influencing, via the astral plane, advanced disciples and inspiring various groups who work for the betterment of humanity. The Buddha, Lord Gautama, taught the transcendental wisdom, while Lord Maitreya teaches through good works, which is why he is also known as the *Bodhisattva*. Study the changes in humanity over that last 40 years; it becomes clear that compassion is a growing phenomenon in various parts of our globe. Humanity has awakened to help the less fortunate in countries beset by natural disasters or negative political regimes. Migrations of people escaping dire circumstances in their own countries are being taken in by more fortunate countries and looked after. More and more people all over the world are more conscious and concerned about the environment, endangered species, and injustices to the animal and plant kingdoms in nature. These are just a couple of examples out of many on how people are now reaching out beyond their borders and creeds to help others. This is the influence of Lord Maitreya as he moves closer to humanity, inspiring people to action.

Tibetan Buddhist teaching says that Lord Maitreya resides somewhere in a place called Tushita heaven, where he still gives discourses on Buddha Dharma to advanced disciples. This is an exoteric explanation regarding Lord Maitreya. The esoteric teaching instead explains that Lord Maitreya is a great being, Master of Masters, who holds all of humanity within his mind, his chittakasha/mental space. "Verily I say unto you, in as much as ye did it unto one of these My brethren, unto one of these least, ye did it unto Me."(9) These are the words of Lord Maitreya as sensed by Mabel Collins when she was taken onto the ethereal spiritual planes by her Master and then told in her book, *Our Glorious Future*, a rare occult work, and a fascinating read. She was an advanced disciple who wrote numerous exceptional occult books that were inspiring and instructive.

Further, I should mention that there are the five 'poisons' which keep man unenlightened and prevent one from finding their true purpose in life. Each poison is related to a Dhyani Buddha who represents the antidote, the way to overcome a particular spiritual hindrance. We had an individual in our group who had issues with anger which is one of the five poisons. Anger is like an explosion of emotional negativity that blasts out and then is gone in a short time. So anger is a psychological expression of instability and erratic behavior. To counter it, this individual would try to feel themselves as Aksobhya Buddha, whose quality is 'unshakable' and whose wisdom is that of the 'great mirror'. Both these qualities counteract the unstable reactions caused by the rising of anger. He would have to become like a mirror that reflects but is untouched by any external action, thus becoming stable and unshakeable. It was a constant battle for him, but in time, as his focusing became stronger, his outbursts began to subside. This is when the meditation on the Dhyani Buddhas starts to become real; a practical work for the aspiring disciple. Through discipline and practical efforts, the five Dhyani Buddhas become a spiritual tool for personal spiritual transformation. The lesson here is that wisdom and victory comes from above.

Life itself is divided into five 'bardo states' or in-between states of existence. The number five figures very strongly in Buddhist philosophy, which also has a strong 5th Ray quality.

So just to review we have

1) Five Dhyani Buddhas
2) Five Manusha Buddhas (historical Buddhas)
3) Five Skandas
4) Five Poisons
5) Five Bardos

In Yoga Vidya or Yoga philosophy the number five again appears

1) Five Vrittis – modifications of the mind (chitta)
2) Five corresponding mental states

Once you really understand this teaching you will recognize that it is really a 5th Ray teaching, an analytical system of mental engineering. The 5th Ray puts this teaching on the mental plane and contemplating on these different attributes can take you to the higher mental plane or to more abstract thought.

The Master Comes

One evening in the spring of 1978, we had a guest over, an Indian gentleman, a Mr. Patel. RN was discussing the sounding of the Great Invocation with him. For some reason, RN told me to go upstairs to the smaller private meditation room and meditate there instead of listening to their discussion. In this second meditation room there was a mandala of Sri Chakra, which RN and his wife had painted, hanging over the altar. The Shiva Lingam had been removed from the altar and was now sitting on a shelf in RN's library. The mandala was striking in a brilliant red and gold combination of colors. I lit an incense stick and the candle and began my meditation. Almost immediately I became frozen in my posture as a force streamed through me from the top of my head down to the base of my spine. It was so intense and powerful, I was filled with awe. I couldn't really tell how long it lasted, maybe only a few minutes, finally I was able to feel and move my body again. Though I didn't see anything, somehow I knew the source. After the experience, I continued with my meditation, focusing on the flame in the heart and chanting for a short time. When I came downstairs, I noticed that our guest had left. Upon seeing me, RN asked about my meditation. I told him what I had experienced and that I felt it was the Master R. He was very surprised and I remember him saying, as we discussed this in the kitchen later, that it made little sense as we had nothing to do with the Master R. As a group we always felt close to the Master D.K. and Master Morya, who is said to be the head of all the occult schools. We knew very little about the Master R, other than what is written in the books of Alice Bailey and a few Theosophical works. A similar experience, like the one I had just gone through, occurred one more time but not with the same intensity.

Shortly after I had these two experiences, RN, his family,

and a couple of group members went down to Virginia Beach for a short vacation. On the way, RN, with his family, stopped to visit some friends in Baltimore. The others continued on to Virginia Beach themselves. That night, as RN told it, the Master R appeared to him in a dream, chanting a mantra in a most unusual way and telling him it was for the group work. RN woke up and woke his daughter up, he chanted the mantra to her and then they both chanted the mantra together. The next morning when RN awoke, he had forgotten the tune for the mantra, but fortunately his daughter remembered it clearly. Then they spent some time chanting together to strengthen their memory of the rhythm and tune of the mantra. At our first group meeting, when RN had returned to Toronto after his family trip, he told us about his dream experience of the Master R and how he received an esoteric tune for one of the mantras we had been chanting. Then he started teaching us how to chant this mantra. The note configuration was so unusual that most of us had difficulty hitting the correct notes when chanting. RN

Lord of the 7th Ray, Master R.
(Painting by author.)

pointed out that one could only truly chant it correctly when they are centered in Essence, this mantra could not be chanted mechanically, as it is truly an esoteric mantra. He said that there is a big difference between just picking any mantra to chant and chanting an esoteric mantra. Anyone can chant a mantra, but its effectiveness is very little, at most it relaxes you and you feel good, whereas with an esoteric mantra the effectiveness is multifaceted and works directly on shifting one's consciousness from the personality to the Essence.

"All these mantrams depend for their potency upon the sound and rhythm and upon the syllabic emphasis imparted to them when enunciating and intoning. They depend, too, upon the capacity of the man who uses them to visualize and to will the desired effect."(10) RN, though untrained in music, had a natural ability to hold a tune. I, on the other hand, had no ability to hold or even distinguish the difference in some of the subtle notes. Thus it took me a long time to learn to chant the mantra with this *esoteric tune* correctly. Actually, it took me several years to really chant the mantra correctly. A mantra has to be chanted with a deep feeling that percolates up from your Essence. As you chant it is necessary to constantly discriminate between Essence feeling and the urges of the personality, otherwise the energy goes in a wrong direction and in time may have adverse effects. That is the real difficulty. With the understanding of mantra came insight into Deity. Mantra does not exist without Deity. Mantra is the fast path that is the key to opening the door to deeper esoteric knowledge.

Not long after receiving this mantra, RN had another dream. In this dream he found himself seated before a colorful, traditional Tibetan painting called a Thanka. His consciousness was focused intensely on this Thanka. Then, from this painting three yogis magically appeared, as if jumping out of the painting. They explained to RN that the mantra, OM Mani Padme Hum, had three levels. One yogi explained that the tune that we were given was the lowest level. Its purpose was fourfold: 1) to awaken the Essence, 2) alignment, 3) purify the bodies and 4) maintain a connection with the inner Ashrams. Then one of the other yogis chanted the tune for the next level. He indicated that this level was only for advanced Initiates and Masters and was very esoteric. The third level, explained by one of the other yogis, was at the level of the Logos and was not for man, but related to the shifting of continents and great changes that happened from time to time on earth. When RN told us this dream, he said the 2nd level chanting was so unusual that he couldn't remember the tune, only that it went from very high notes, dropping down to lower notes, then back to higher notes. He felt that this dream was given to him to convince him of the power and importance of the mantra as he was still clinging somewhat to the mantra of Lord Shiva. He also pointed out that this dream showed him that the more advanced the individual who was chanting, the less amount of chants were required to get the expected results. Previously, he said, he was under the impression that one had to chant a mantra hundreds of times to get results. At the most advanced level or 'para mantra' the mantra would only have to be repeated two or three times as was indicated in his dream. RN said that this helped him to totally break with his clinging. This in itself was a minor initiation for RN.

Our group meetings became focused on learning to chant the mantra correctly. We had to sustain our focus and visualization, while trying to generate or create a deep feeling within, plus maintain vocal harmony with the entire group as we chanted. All this had to be done at the same time. One time we were sitting in the main meeting room in a circle, chanting intensely, during the day, for more than 40 minutes. Then the front door bell rang; RN motioned for me to see who it was. When I had done that and returned to the room where the group was still chanting, as I neared the circle, I distinctly felt as if I was entering through a force field, from outside to inside. RN later explained that our chanting was creating a 'cone of fire' which not only protected the group, but also allowed for the downpour of energy from the higher planes. What we found out later was that this cone of fire was actually the work of the Devas that are attracted by the chanting and they build, so to speak, this cone of fire. These Devas are also related to the esoteric school that we belonged to. They are the Devas of Avalokiteshvara. There are great Devas that are on the same advanced level as a Master of Wisdom, they all work together. The Deva evolution is a parallel evolution to man but on the ethereal realms of existence. When an individual, or more so a group, begins to make progress on the Path, then these Devas will begin to help in the effort. If much greater progress is made then the Devas may contact an individual or members of a group (see chapter on the advent of the Devas).

Psychic Artist

When RN and family had gone to Virginia Beach, they visited the Edgar Cayce Center. RN's wife was very attracted to Cayce's work. While visiting there and attending a lecture, they met some fascinating people and invited them to Toronto. One lady, I'll call her Elizabeth, was a pastor at a small alternative church in Wisconsin and had a very unusual story. She decided to come and visit us and actually stayed with us for over a week. Several years back, Elizabeth got into an argument with her husband while driving him in their car. He was sitting in the back seat at the time. The argument made him so angry that he lost control of himself and struck her hard in the back of the head with his cane. The strange end result was that Elizabeth became very psychic. Her unusual ability was that she could sit in a darkened room, totally dark, and draw a psychic portrait of her subject. She used pastels on a special textured paper. These portraits were remarkable, as they were so life like that the eyes seemed to look back at you.

We all wanted Elizabeth to do our psychic portraits. These portraits, Elizabeth pointed out, were of how your Higher self might look. Once the portrait was finished, the lights would be turned on and Elizabeth would explain what she had seen about you in a spiritual sense. She also mentioned that you might notice, over time, that these portraits might seem to change. Elizabeth did not have any artistic training at all. This talent just awakened after the incident with her now ex-husband.

From this experience everyone in the group learned something of importance about their own spiritual path. The room felt so silent and still, although I could hear Elizabeth drawing quickly as I sat motionless in total darkness. I have to admit that my psychic portrait was not what I had expected. The portrait was of a bearded, quite bald, older man. I didn't look Buddhist. Made me think of a rabbi! Yet there was an intensity and strength in the eyes. Elizabeth said that I had a capacity for deep meditation and that I had worked at meditation in my past lives, but that I was weak in dealing with general life circumstances. Even RN had his portrait done. Then he asked Elizabeth if she could do a portrait of the group. He didn't mean a group portrait in the sense of a group photograph, but a psychic picture of any of the forces being invoked by the group. The result was most unusual! The portrait came out showing a man with a second head coming out of the main head. This of course awakened our curiosity as it seemed so bizarre. She called this individual that she had drawn, 'Master Challenger'. She said the group was making progress but forces were gathering to test the group. Forces of a very psychic nature, but she couldn't see details of how these tests would manifest. This Master Challenger came sooner rather than later!

Aspirants on the Path of Return are always tested once they start making progress. This is a Law of the Path. It cannot be avoided. These tests come through natural karmic causes. Such tests always strike at one's weaknesses, where you're vulnerable, unsure of yourself, and where there are underlining fears. They are there to test the determination, perseverance, sincerity, and strength of the neophyte. The Master D.K. talks about the tests of the Probationary Path that gauge the aspirants' strength, perseverance and dedication to the upward Way. Once you pass through this stage, the tests of the accepted disciple are of a much more subtle nature, especially once you've seen the face of the *Dweller on the Threshold* and enter the Path of Initiation.

Tapas – Super Effort

As part of our group Work, we started to focus on Full Moon meditations, especially the Full Moon of WESAK. The Master D.K. had mentioned in several of the books by Alice Bailey that WESAK is a very significant event. To escalate the power of the Full Moon and to prepare for WESAK, RN introduced us to an aspect of yoga called 'tapas'. Tapas is a form of yogic discipline that is mentioned in the Yoga Sutras as a means to 'fan the inner flame' of aspiration. Gurdjieff calls this increased effort 'super effort'. This super effort is also a means to test yourself, see what you're made of, or how strong you are in a spiritual sense. When done in a group environment, the added support really encourages you to make the effort needed and to do your best. One thing about 'tapas', once a tapas has been set, it must be completed. Never devise tapas that are greater than the abilities of those who are going to take part.

We did various types of 'tapas' over the years, from very simple to more complex. A simpler, short 'tapas' was to sit down and read for one hour while not moving at all and holding the feeling of the flame in the heart. Sounds simple until you try it! No moving means NO MOVING. Not even moving to scratch that itch that's bugging you while you sit.

Many aspirants who meditate regularly find that you lose the feeling and composure that meditation gives you when you go to work and deal with the rigors of daily life. When you are at work, your focus is on your job. Consequently, your early morning meditation experience already seems like a distant memory, it's far away. Even the ideas of the Work seem to slip away during the workday hours. Thus RN devised a 'tapas' for the group to help overcome this difficulty and to increase inner awareness throughout the day. The tapas was simple; for three days of the Full Moon period we would fast, only eating three apples a day (you could drink as much water as you needed) plus drinking three cups of tea. Everyone would start the tapas at 8 a.m. then each one of us had to focus and visualize the inner flame and sound the mantra six times (either silent or aloud, depending on where you were) every hour on the hour. The daily tapas would end at 8 p.m. but you still had to do your regular daily meditations.

The purpose of this particular tapas was two-fold in nature. It was to put pressure on the appetites of one's body, on your awareness, and to be alert mentally in order to do the chanting each hour. For me, at the time I was a high school teacher, many times the classes would be changing every hour so I had a few free minutes to focus and chant. It was much easier when my workday was over, usually around 3:30 p.m., so I didn't have to deal with too many external activities. Yet one time, just when school was over, I was rushing to catch a bus to get to the garage where my car was being repaired. As I was rushing down the sidewalk, I felt like a force hit me with the thought to look at my watch. It was exactly 4 p.m., time to focus to do the tapas. I had almost missed the 'on the hour' discipline, fortunately this force or inner guide wasn't going to let me and I received a psychic reminder. This really startled me! My personality was focused on catching the bus and getting my car but my Essence was focused on the tapas.

At the end of the three days, the group would get together to meditate, and to break the fast, enjoying some fruit and sweets while comparing notes and experiences.

Astral Forces

Doing these disciplines or tapas seemed to bring the group closer together and increased the group energy. Things started to happen! One night an electrical wire broke and was dancing around outside the house, creating a cascade of sparks. It was quite a light show. At the same time the mandala of Shri-Chakra, hanging over the upstairs altar, fell down. Strange noises like snaps on the walls in the house were heard all at the same time. RN said he felt that a Devic force was now encompassing the house. Most of us didn't really understand what that meant but the display of phenomena was exciting. The Master D.K. mentions in his teaching that psychic phenomena is of little importance and being glamorized by it could in fact slow the aspirant down in their quest for esoteric knowledge. Such phenomena was an expression of astral forces, the Master D.K. pointed out, and the aspirant had to achieve a mental stability first before exploring the astral world of phenomena. The group had done a lot of reading on the early days of the Theosophical Society and the phenomena that surrounded Helena Blavatsky. She used such phenomena, like flowers spontaneously dropping from the ceiling, during her talks to help convince would be aspirants of the Victorian age that there was more than just the visible world. But those exhibitions seemed to create cynicism and distrust instead of faith. The Masters abandoned that course of action and there is almost no mention of psychic phenomena in the same sense in the years following Helena Blavatsky's death. In *The Voice of the Silence*, a passage states, "...thy Soul will find the blossoms of life but under every flower a serpent coiled." (11) This is a subtle warning of the dangers of the astral plane. The student of esoteric wisdom first must ground themselves thoroughly by integrating the arcane teaching with their entire body, heart and mind. By developing mental concepts based on the principles of the teaching they act as a safeguard, helping to awaken 'viveka' or spiritual discrimination between the 'real and the unreal'. In this way you rise above the 'astral', aligning with the higher mental plane and awakening true intuition, thus interest in astral phenomena drops away.

Raja Yoga, Pratyahara: The Key to Yogic Meditation

Because the understanding of the principles of the Work, or 'Work ideas' is so important, in the group meeting we always read sections from books or discussed the books we were studying. We spent a lot of time reading and discussing *Letters on Occult Meditation*, then we worked to apply the instructions that the Master D.K. gave out with utmost care. One of the key ideas of occult meditation is laid out right at the beginning of the book. The idea of alignment is central to understanding and entering into deeper levels of meditation. The Master D.K. applies the knowledge from the Yoga Sutras and words it in a way that Western readers can get some insight into the process of alignment. In the Yoga Sutras, alignment is called 'pratyahara'. The yogis understood 'pratyahara' as the state of withdrawing all the forces that are in constant motion to a *'point of focus'* or tension, detaching from the outer world of the senses. Then if you're meditating and there is a lot of noise or disturbances, you are not disturbed by it. Sometime while we were meditating, RN would take two small blocks of wood and smash them together making a very sharp noise. He would watch to see who would jump from the sudden loud noise. If you didn't move, then your meditation was proceeding well. I mentioned before that we focused on the flame, visualizing our bodies as hollow and empty. We would also, at the same time, see that we are not our empty hollow body, not our emotions, neither happy nor sad, and not our thoughts. Focusing on the flame we would ponder for a minute or two, mentally feeling that we are, *"an Eternal Soul, a Sacred Flame within the greater Divine Flame"*. Once we were focused and aligned, with our bodies quiet, then we were ready to chant. Another term for alignment is *'centering'*. Visualizing the flame as a focal point of tension provides the means to achieve centering or alignment. This idea of centering and alignment is also visually indicated in the *Labours of Hercules* in Cancer, where Hercules must catch the little fawn and hold it close to his heart and offer it onto the altar of Apollo.

From the classical yogic tradition, meditation, which in Sanskrit is called *'dhyana'*, is not achieved until the yogi can become accomplished in the ability of withdrawing the attention inward (pratyahara), then attain true, unwavering, one-pointed concentration (dharana) after which comes the stage of dhyana or meditation.

In our group efforts we worked on different forms of meditation, like <u>Koan</u> practice of Zen, the 'Light and the Dust' of the Pure Land Buddhist school and other occult methods. In the 4th Way teaching this same idea is expressed through the idea of developing a *'center of gravity'*. When you first experience the place of your center of gravity, you feel the flow of force pulling you back, deeper into the feeling of the space of the 'I-am'. Once this is accomplished continually, then eventually you crystallize this 'point of tension', the Essential Nature.

Even though the forms of meditation may differ, in essence, they all provide the opportunity for the same type of practice for achieving alignment. In the group we used the term 'centered' or in 'Essence'. If you are not 'in Essence', it means that you are no longer within the group aura; instead you would now be pushed out onto the periphery of the group. What does that mean? The Work is sometimes called, 'Great Sifter'. Just like panning for gold, the miner has to sift out the slag or sand, stones and debris, leaving the gold. The power of the Group Work is very similar. The negative aspects of

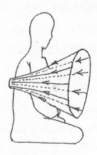

Diagram is showing how to develop a 'center of gravity' through focusing on a point of tension and then drawing all forces to that point.

the personality have to be 'sifted out' leaving behind the gold, the Essence. This is a big, long process.

As I mentioned before, the Essence is a reflection of the Soul on its own plane as the soul in incarnation. When an individual begins to question about life and search for something more, looking at various philosophies, religions, or alternative life styles, that means that the Soul has reached a certain stage in its evolution and it begins to stir its reflection, the soul in incarnation, into action, to search. Initially though, the search for truth, the deeper mysteries of life begins with the thought-life of the personality, which is based on subconscious past life memories. For instance, a soul born into a Jewish family all of a sudden drops their traditions and becomes Buddhist. I know one family of four siblings, where three of the brothers left their birth religion, Judaism, and became Buddhist. Why does such an event occur? Is it a problem of their religion or their parents? Psychologists and social service workers would come up with many answers, from peer group pressures, exotic adventure, or the lack of practicality of the old traditions and many more. Gaining an understanding of the laws of rebirth or reincarnation and karma would make understanding the situation of this family discernible. These three young men had strong Buddhist roots from the distant past. They had incarnated together in the same family. Because Buddhism was becoming popular at that time, first the older brother came in contact with some Buddhist influence that awakened this old, unconscious memory but it was strong enough to cause him to make a big life change. The same happened with the other, younger, brothers. From the occult perspective, the old personality or 'kama-rupa' made up of 'samskaras' from the past, replaced the present personality, thus the personality that 'felt' or 'identified' with being Jewish had withdrawn and the old Buddhist personality had re-awakened. Today this is more common than you think.

The Sanskrit word, '<u>Samskara'</u>, is used by the Buddhist and

Hindu yogic traditions, its meaning is 'talents or tendencies'. These talents and tendencies lie hidden in the subconscious mind. A good example is a child prodigy, who displays some special talent at a very young age with no apparent source. The source is the distant past. Science today knows that energy cannot be destroyed only redirected. All our life, through our constant activity as humans, we generate energy. When we die, this energy is transferred from the coarse physical body to a more subtle body, the astral body, which also dies and the energy again is transferred and stored in the body of the Soul or Causal body, in the permanent atoms which act like a hard disk drive, storing the essence of all life's events over a vast period of time. This opens an area of important investigation, the study of the Soul.

When light increases the shadows become more apparent. As the aspirant makes progress and begins to sense the voice of the Soul, the Path appears to become steeper and the climb much more strenuous and one's footing becomes unsure.

There are two paths

1) Path of least resistance, and
2) Path of greatest resistance.

The path of least resistance is the 'way of the personality', or as the Master D.K. puts it, the way of the 'lunar lords or pitris'. Gurdjieff calls this the mechanical life of Man #1, #2, and #3. The group spent several years working with these ideas, not to achieve an intellectual understanding, but instead, a practical working knowledge of what these lofty ideas meant on a day-to-day basis. For fun, I made t-shirts for the entire group with a picture of the Enneagram with the title, <u>Man #4</u>. This simple designation of Man #1, 2 and so forth is a unique approach to seeing the human condition on this planet. Briefly, Man #1, 2, and 3 relate to the masses of humanity, either controlled by

A) Physical bodies

B) Emotions (astral)

C) Intellect (lower mind)

If you look at the masses of humanity, the vast majority of people earn their living via their physical bodies: construction workers, farmers, miners, sports professionals, warehouse personal, shippers/receivers, firemen, rescue operations, military and so many more. These are called Man #1. The next section, Man #2, although there are many, they are not as abundant as Man #1. People who are Man #2 are ruled by their emotions: artists, musicians, housewife/mother, poets, daycare worker, actor, and others. Next, Man #3 is conditioned by the lower mind, the intellectual center. In this group we have professors, lawyers, doctors, engineers, novelists, teachers, journalists, politicians and some others but in this group there are far less people than the other two groups. Now, remember that this is a generalization which acts only as a guide. There are overlaps, for instance, a sports professional or actor becoming a politician. Dancers can be a combination, still strong Man #1 but with a taste of Man #2. The other point to remember is that there is no difference on an evolutionary spiritual level between Man #1, 2, and 3. This is what Gurdjieff called 'mechanical humanity'. The change begins with Man #4. That's why I made the Man #4 t-shirts.

Man #4 is the aspirant, the seeker after something more than what society offers. Our group was made up of seekers aspiring to become Man #5. There are many stages that the aspirant to the Divine Mysteries has to pass through during the stage of Man #4. In Buddhism, Man #4 is called, 'strotapatti', the 'stream enterer'. In esoteric Christianity it is the Baptism. If you study the esoteric tradition of many teachings, in time, you will find a correlation between them all. The stories in the Bible are taken literally by many, but in fact, there are various esoteric teachings hidden there if your eyes are open to see them. For our group to become

Man #4 meant to awaken to one's Essential Nature and realize for a fact that this Essence is separate from the personality but also works through it. To make this idea a reality takes years of effort, many trials and in some cases, ordeals, for the group members as they worked to transfer their feeling of 'I-ness' identification from the personality, an expression of kama-manas, to the Essence. In fact, that's what the esoteric work is all about.

It is this effort, the constant exertion to awaken the Essence that leads to the portal of the Esoteric Path. Perseverance in this focused exertion causes the aspirant to come face to face with different forces and energies within, which must be made conscious then faced and transformed, creating a focused harmony within one's total being. Then the aspirant, now becoming a disciple, may learn one of the deep esoteric secrets which are only hinted at in some esoteric books. A separation takes place between the aspirant as Essence, the personality, and the 'Dweller on the Threshold'. This is where the danger lies and that is why it is so important to have a teacher who has been through this and knows what to look for to help the student.

Meditation alone is not enough, but it is the backbone of spiritual discipline. Study is also very important as it acts as an anchor to keep the aspirant from letting the mind get caught in fantasy and dreaming about enlightenment. Study, in fact, is an important step in one's meditation effort as it helps to redirect the thought activity from mundane, mechanical, worldly thoughts, to pondering on higher, more abstract thoughts, builds in new ideas to replace old ideas, and creates a springboard to inspiration. When studying it's important to focus on a spiritual tradition which has produced awakened, enlightened Masters who can act as a guidepost or even a teacher when one isn't present at the time. Quality of study is important, not quantity. Don't rush through books just to have them read. Don't try to memorize, you're not preparing for a test. Underlining and taking notes is helpful. Make notes on your own from your understanding, not copying from the book. Meditate and ponder on the ideas that you're reading about. It is necessary to make the ideas 'yours'. This takes time and comes from applying the various spiritual/esoteric doctrines in daily life.

Rules of the Group Work

In the group we worked hard, but also had our enjoyments. In the summer months we would go on picnics, swim and hike, enjoying the beautiful scenery and nature north of the city. Even when sitting under a shady tree and enjoying our picnic lunch, our conversation would inevitably turn to discussions of the Work, or we would read excerpts from a book and then discuss it. This seemed to make our outings even more enjoyable. Sometimes we would do silent group meditations. One time we sat in silence, just focusing on the flame in our hearts, listening to the sounds of nature, trying to feel nature from our inner most being. Nature does have a sound, sometimes that sound is a feeling of a deep silence and harmony.

The group Work is a dynamic undertaking, unlike in bygone times when aspirants would follow a singular path and retire into a retreat, today's group work takes place within the hustle and bustle of the city. In the group you have a variety of different personalities that interact with each other on a regular basis. The group doesn't just sit quietly in meditation and then listen to a reading. Maybe in the beginning, but as the group work evolved we became a big family. Life in a family is not static, as the personalities interact, points of friction or divergence will arise. "In the group, meditation leads to the fusion of the group personnel, to their united invocative appeal, and – when invocation has evoked response – it leads to group receptivity to that which has been spiritually demanded, and thus to the spiritual service of the group". (12) It is the resolving of these tensions that becomes the Group Work. In the group there are rules, not many rules, but they must be understood and followed, otherwise the group will fall to pieces.

The Group Rules:

1) No negative emotions
2) Discipline must be maintained (daily meditation, study)
3) Attendance at all meetings is required
4) Share with your group members.

Of these four rules, #1 is the most difficult to understand and apply.

What does 'no negative emotions' mean? First of all, negative emotions are very destructive, they destroy marriages, friendships, and any other type of relationship. The disciple must be careful not to express negative emotions, and even to guard against their silent repetition within the mind. In the group environment 'gossip' is the first negative emotion that must be silenced. Gossip is an immature reflection of jealousy and envy, two very strong negative emotions. In Buddhism both jealousy and envy are considered a major hindrance on the path. In spiritual groups members become jealous of others if they hear the teacher praising one member and not them. Then others feel left out or they assume the other member must be making progress faster on the path than they are. Then they start to look for faults in that individual, and before long they're gossiping with other members, pulling others into the vortex of negativity. When your eyes open on the esoteric path, you will soon see that such negativity creates a 'group dweller', which becomes like a thick fog or 'glamour', using the Master D.K.'s terminology, in which the group soon can lose its way or even break up. Another negative emotion which is destructive is arrogance. Many times, one or two members of a group feel they know more than the other members and become arrogant, talking down to the other members. This causes tensions between members, breaking down the harmony in the group. In larger groups such behavior results in small factions forming within the group. This is why it's necessary to have a strong, awakened teacher, who will see the play of negative emotions and quickly stop them from getting out of hand.

The Esoteric Path is not based on democracy but instead is hierarchical, with a teacher at its head. What does this mean? The idea of hierarchy is a universal archetype that is prevalent throughout our planet, though few people see it as it is. Governments, industry, religions and organizations are all based on a hierarchical system. Even democracies still have a hierarchy, the prime minister and his cabinet are the core, then the House of Commons or in the US, the President, his main advisors, then Congress and Senate. Though we don't politically define it as a hierarchy, it is in fact based on the same archetypical structure. Religious organizations are seen as more hierarchical, with the Pope and the school of Cardinals, or the Dali Lama and his close Lama advisers. So it is with spiritual groups. The guru and maybe a few advanced disciples would hold the other disciples and the business of the ashram together. Religion has done away with the idea of an invisible spiritual hierarchy and focuses just on the belief in God. The esoteric tradition posits that there is a Spiritual Hierarchy of enlightened immortal Beings, who have a definite relationship with the overall welfare of this planet. This hierarchy doesn't interfere with the 'free will' of the individual, but acts as a 'Guardian Wall' to protect the planet from outside or cosmic malevolence and also inspires, guides, and uplifts those members of humanity who have the welfare of humankind at their heart. There is a symbiotic relationship between the Spiritual Hierarchy and all life on this planet.

RN was our spiritual or occult teacher, not a guru. He told us that he was the intermediary teacher whose task was to prepare us to reach that point where we would be centered in Essence, enabling us to recognize our real guru when the time comes. RN was spiritually more advanced than any of the members of the group. His knowledge of esoteric traditions both East and West was, to us, mind boggling, plus he had an uncanny knack for knowing our spiritual psychological state on a day-to-day basis. As the group evolved, so did RN. Certain events occurred which propelled the group and RN deeper into the esoteric world.

The Work to Come

There were major and minor events which actually gave a picture of things to come. One such event involved my cousin, who was visiting from England, a student of G.I.Gurdjieff, studying primarily the special movements he had develop to awaken the aspirant. She was also interested in what we were doing, so I introduced her to RN. RN was very interested in seeing the Gurdjieff movements. One night she joined us in our meditation. RN asked her to sit in the center of our meditation circle where she could do the movements created by Gurdjieff. Though I could see her body twisting and turning in an odd fashion but I wasn't able to see psychically what was happening to her. The room felt electric as she did what is suppose to be an esoteric dance, in what appeared to be like slow motion. As she did the movements, the group chanted in unison, and then at one point a strange clanging sound was suddenly heard, it was quite loud. RN said that something had just come out of her, pulled out by the group chanting. She said she now felt less tension inside her after this experience. At this time we weren't sure what it was that came out of her. This was like an exorcism of some kind. Little did we know at the time what this would lead up too!

Then there was the young girl, Shirley, who I mentioned before, that asked me about the word 'atma' which she had seen in a dream. She had started coming to the group meetings on the weekend. We found out later that her father was very against her coming, and she was literally sneaking away to come to our center. One day, the group was sitting around the table discussing a book, *Regents of the 7 Spheres*, and RN mentioned that one of the pictures in the book was the Deva form of the Master Serapis. RN passed the book around for us to see the picture. When Shirley looked at the picture, she immediately swooned, falling on the floor. RN picked her up and put her head on his lap. He said she had gone into a type of trance, that this was not a normal fainting. RN rang a small Tibetan bell and chanted a mantra very softly close to her ear and Shirley awoke. She couldn't really tell us what she experienced, other than she felt far away and in the presence of her Master, enclosed in an envelope of a loving, uplifting feeling. At the same time several of the other group members, including myself, experienced a radiant, golden, whirling light. RN said that it was the Deva form of the Master Serapis manifesting. Shirley must be a very advanced soul, we asked? RN said that she was, as she was drawn to the Work at such a young age. None of us were sure who our Master was, and now this young girl did.

Dweller on the Threshold

Before I venture further in the story of Shirley, there is another very esoteric subject that needs some elucidation. The nature of this topic only allows for a brief description. It is too esoteric for the printed page and there are only a couple of books that hint at this topic in an esoteric sense. It has to do with the 'Dweller on the Threshold'. This is an occult term to describe the totality of negative personality characteristics that have accumulated over many, many past lives that become the overall restricting obstacle to entering the Path of Initiation. Terms such as 'shadow', 'kama-rupa', 'namdog', 'kleasa' or 'the nether personality' are some other names of this element within the occult constitution of man. The soul, when it is advanced enough, causes an inner separation between the Essence, (soul in incarnation) Personality and the DOTH (Dweller on the Threshold). This separation occurs gradually, in most cases, but as the Essence starts to awaken the DOTH becomes a separate existence situated on the astral plane. In the book *Zanoni* by Sir Edward Bulwer Lytton, Glyndon, the young aspirant, undergoes the initial tests of the threshold of an ancient occult order that Mejnour, his teacher, belongs to. Glyndon fails in his first major test of trust and patience and is cast out of the school. Unfortunately, Glyndon has gone too far and awakened the 'fiend', as it is called in the book, the DOTH. When Glyndon is more in his Essence, he sees this 'thing', as separate from him but tied to his aura. This story has some major clues about the DOTH. Mejnour, in the book, is a no nonsense teacher, very 5th Ray, like a pure scientist, without any emotional attachment to his students. He knows the occult laws, and if you break these unwritten inner occult rules, he instantly ends the teacher/student relationship and you're out of the school. The Essence must learn to see and feel itself as separate from both the personality and also the negative force of the DOTH. The DOTH appears to have a life of its own, until the Essence, using the personality, can control it, and then in time, eliminate it. Zanoni, in the book, teaches Glyndon that when you face this dreaded fiend, looking at it eye to eye, it will shrink and lose its power. You can't do this unless you have achieved a certain level of separation and soul strength and awakening.

In the poem, *Green Leaves, Words from the Master*, the DOTH is that 'heavy iron bar that clasps and holds the golden gate' which the neophyte must lift. The type of DOTH which an aspirant to the Path of Initiation may experience is dependent on one's actions in the distant past. If an individual has practiced black magic in ancient times, then those entities that were drawn to him in that dark past will still be there, and would make up the substance aspect of the DOTH. The aspirant will have to deal with them and transform their substance before the Essence, the true inner disciple, can go further. This point is explained very well in the book, *The Wheel of Rebirth* by H.K. Chalonner. In the chapter on England, Charles re-awakens his occult past and realizes that his cancer is the result of an ancient elemental, an entity create by magic that lives in his aura, that must now be dissolved before he can make further progress on the Path. The classic occult volume, *Light on the Path* by Mabel Collins, describes the DOTH as '...it is a plant that lives and increases throughout the ages. It flowers when the man has accumulated unto himself innumerable existences. He who will enter upon the path of power must tear this thing out of his heart'. (13)

Another way to explore the topic of the DOTH is to consider some of the ideas from the 4th Way. Self-observation is the key that begins to unlock the door to the mysteries. But self-observation can be either passive or active. Most students do self-observation passively, that is, they do observe different aspects of themselves but leave it at that. To make self-observation active, you have to concretize what you've seen by first writing down your observations, then categorizing, and finally studying your observation. An easy way to start is by creating four categories

1) Essence characteristics.
2) Negative personality traits.
3) Positive personality traits.
4) Neutral personality traits.

The difficulty here is that you have to be absolutely truthful about yourself. How many people are? Thus once you've made your findings, it's best to bring them out in a group meeting for discussion. This is where the group work becomes tested. This Work must be guided by a teacher who can see through the miasma of personality. The other group members taking part must attempt to be in Essence, not in their personality. It is very important that negative emotions not be allowed to creep into this type of work effort. It takes time to be able to really be successful at the discipline of self-observation. Being able to differentiate between Essence and personality is in itself a major task that requires a keen eye and an awakened spiritual discrimination (viveka). Since we are discussing the DOTH it's important to watch those voices, the inner voices that are resistant to this exercise, especially when presenting to the group. That's when you really observe yourself. Those voices of resistance, fear (I wish it was over) and doubt (this is not necessary) are the tip of an iceberg, this is just the DOTH sticking up its head, just becoming visible.

In the books of Alice A. Bailey that give out the esoteric teaching of the Tibetan Master D.K., there is in *Esoteric Astrology* a definition of the DOTH: "this Dweller is the sum total of all the personality characteristics which have remained unconquered and unsubdued and which must be finally overcome before initiation can be taken".(14) In *A Treatise on White Magic*, the Tibetan Master says further, "the light first throws into relief and brings into the foreground of consciousness those thought-forms and entities which depict the lower life, and which (in their aggregate) form the Dweller on the Threshold".(15) In fact, in the esoteric sense, the un-awakened personality is the Dweller. When you awaken 'that' which is what awakens, the soul in incarnation, the Essence, it intensifies soul light, and the Dweller on the Threshold becomes visible, and the battle on the astral plane, Kurushretra, really begins. It's as if a darkened room has a low wattage light bulb, all the contents may be visible but not so clearly – that's how we see life – on the other hand, if a very powerful, high wattage light bulb is used, not only are the objects in the room seen in a more distinct manner, but many shadows are also cast.

Now for a couple of practical directions of what happens when the DOTH awakens and the battle rages. Remember, this awakening occurs in stages, step by step. The DOTH is like a balloon. When the aspirant identifies with negative thoughts and emotions and loses the feeling of their Essence, then the Essence energy/shakti leaks out to the DOTH, causing the balloon to inflate, rapidly increasing the power and size of the DOTH. The Essence then gets temporarily covered up, instantly becoming powerless and the DOTH becomes very active and controlling. When this occurs it's a crucial moment, where the struggling aspirant must make an intense all-out effort to find their deeper *'feeling'* and center back in Essence. *You cannot think your way out.* Too often, aspirants spend too much time trying to understand what's happening to them. Why is this happening to me? Whose fault is it? Am I on the right path? So many questions can enter into your mind when this happens. All the thoughts you now experience are from the DOTH and they are wrong. At first this is very hard to grasp. Your feeling of Essence-self is absorbed by this DOTH, thus you cannot see correctly what your spiritual or Essence state is. The DOTH will always project thoughts that pump up the 'five poisons' (arrogance, anger, greed, jealousy, and self-pity/depression) depending on which one is the weak point in your character.

The DOTH always wants to run away from the group work, thinking that you can do it yourself, the group isn't right for you, the teacher is unfair or biased, favoring other group members, and the list goes on and on. Also the DOTH will always find faults with the teacher, thus creating doubts about the purpose and legitimacy of the Work, adding more reasons why it is necessary to run away. What most aspirants don't realize is that the DOTH will always kill any true feelings of love. The DOTH is always destructive, first to your soul, then to those closest to you. The DOTH makes you numb so you cannot feel. The DOTH is like a thick fog but you're not conscious that you're lost in the fog, "it is the shadow of thyself outside the Path...".(16) That's why it is a matter of paramount importance that the teacher himself has passed this stage and can guide you through the maze of illusions created by the DOTH. Feeling love, devotion (bhakti) and surrender is the antidote. But when you're trapped in the dark folds of the DOTH's embrace, you cannot feel, so your feeling of love or 'bhakti' is frozen. If you're fortunate to have a teacher with some occult power who can help crack through some of this dark matter and help liberate the Essence from the DOTH's grip, then one's 'bhakti' or love can flow again. In most cases it's up to the aspirant to learn over time to deal with this problem on their own, developing perseverance, inner strength, and strong faith in the higher forces of Light. This is probably why the Master D.K. mentions that the period between the 1st Initiation and the 2nd Initiation is the hardest and longest for the aspirant, sometimes taking up to seven lifetimes. The DOTH isn't 100 percent dissolved until the 4th Initiation. At the 3rd Initiation the DOTH is more in a dormant state although it has been cleaned out, but there remains a kernel of its existence that can actually come back to life. The Path to Liberation is very different than what's shown in the majority of spiritual books, as they never touch on the subject of the Dweller on the Threshold.

Now going back to Shirley, she had an advanced Essence, but because of the higher group energy and the force of her Master, it turned out that her DOTH separated and was very large and had Egyptian characteristics, meaning she had practiced magic in that distant past. Her Master, The Master Serapis, was an Egyptian from the School of Luxor. Because of the high group energy, this little girl then underwent a dramatic change which became very visible. A forceful, arrogant, controlling personality emerged at times. When RN, Joanne and Fred came to visit me in India, Shirley literally tried to take over the group while we were away. Fortunately, Shirley had a strong love for RN, so when he returned he was able to help her learn to control this aspect of her dweller. Shortly after this, Shirley's DOTH reasserted itself and when RN chanted with her he experienced huge negative forces around her that seemed to envelop him. RN had to chant with the group for many hours over a couple of days to break through this mass of living, negative astral substance. This task of cleaning Shirley out became a massive effort which went on for several months. Eventually Shirley left the group. Even with RN's and the group's help, the forces around her were very powerful, controlling her every thought and she eventually wanted to break away. We couldn't stop her, she was very young and other aspects of her life were awakening. RN was told by the Master Serapis that she would be okay but she would not make further occult progress in this life. Her 'dweller' was very powerful, charged with Egyptian magic. This experience was an eye opener for all of us and as a group we realized that we had just entered into an area of occult experience not indicated in books. I bumped into Shirley years later and could see that her life had normalized; she had a good job, was married but didn't pursue any further occult teaching. When we talked about general things she was all smiles and friendly, but when we started to talk about the group and the past I could feel a heaviness descend around me and I quickly changed the topic of conversation. The danger of her ancient past was still alive and around her. That was the last time I saw Shirley.

Second Trip to India

Not long after this, RN said I should go to India to practice intense meditation on my own, and that I should stay in Darjeeling. The Master D.K. mentions in one of his books that Darjeeling, on the inner planes, is one of the chakras of the earth.

Mt. Kangchenjunga as seen from Darjeeling,
(photo by author)

Darjeeling is a hill station with one of the best mountain views in the world. Kangchenjunga, the third highest mountain in the world, spans across the complete horizon with a chain of Trans-Himalayan snow-capped mountains stretching as far as the eye can see, giving the beholder an amazing panoramic view.

Previously I mentioned that RN, myself and a couple of group members had gone to India. Actually, I had been there already for some time and RN and the other two group members came later to visit me and then we travelled together for a month. I met up with them at the Bombay (Mumbai) airport and we stayed in a hotel in Juhu Beach, which is about 45 minutes outside of

Bombay. The next day we headed to Elora to meditate in the caves there. Unlike me when I was there three years previously, RN would stand as we meditated in the central Buddhist cave. We spent three days there meditating and touring the area. During one of our meditation sessions, RN said there was a presence of a yogi behind us for a short time. He said this yogi, whoever he was, changed the octave or the note of our esoteric mantra and helped charge it with more shakti, spiritual energy. RN was the only one who sensed this spiritual happening. We also took a road trip for a couple of hours and went to see the caves at Ajunta one afternoon. They were more beautiful and the sculptures more elaborate than those at the Elora caves, but they did not have the spiritual feeling that we all clearly felt at Elora. Also the caves at Ajunta were crowded with noisy tourists, whereas the Elora caves were quiet and serene, and there were very few tourists. We felt that Elora must have some invisible occult protection in order to maintain its spiritual essence.

Next we all went to south India to Adyar, and stayed one night at the Theosophical Society's headquarters. The headquarters of the TS was right on the Indian Ocean, with a large beach front. It was like a peaceful oasis. We enjoyed our stay and they even had 'afternoon tea'. RN and I had an unusual occult experience that night. I was sharing a room with RN, and in the middle of the night he woke me up saying we had to meditate immediately. He said he was being attacked by a powerful evil force that seemed to put him in an astral straight jacket or cage. To intensify the power of the meditation we visualized one of the Masters above us, creating a triangle. We chanted and chanted, holding our focus, maintaining this occult triangle of power. Finally RN said that the negative force had lifted. He said it was a Dugpa, a left-hand path force that was blanketing the Theosophical Society here at Adyar, preventing it from continuing to be an effective spiritual force in the world. This negative force, really a dark force, didn't like us meditating there as we created a disturbance in the astral, so to speak, which threatened it, so it attacked us.

RN had felt a strong pull to go to the Nilgiri Hills, so when we left the TS we took a local bus to Kotagiri which was not too far from Adyar. One of the great Master Yogis of India, sometimes known as the 'Old Man of the South' or the 'Regent of India', was rumored to live somewhere in the Nilgiri Hills. This great Master was mentioned briefly in certain Theosophical texts which indicated that he was a great astrologer. He also went by the name, 'Master Jupiter'. He was a very mysterious Master, who had lived for untold years. We arrived in the Nilgiri Hills and stayed in Kotagiri for a couple of nights. RN said he could sense this great Master but didn't tell us much more, except that he was to go to an old temple which was standing on top of one of the hills, not too far from where we were staying. He said he was told that there was supposed to be the ruins of an ancient temple of a great bhakti, known as Runga Nada, a mysterious yogi, and we had to find it. We eventually found a guide who took us there, guiding us on a long trek through dense forests and up a very steep hill. On the top was just the lower part of a wall. It must have been a very small temple as only a floor area was visible. Someone had kept a crude altar. I was expecting something a little more interesting to investigate. RN said that he felt some familiarity with this little temple and that's where the initials 'RN' came from.

After travelling to a few other spiritual 'hot spots', RN and I went to Calcutta (Kolkata) while the other two members headed to Arunachala to meditate on the holy mountain. Calcutta is a very large, densely populated city, where thousands of people still live on the street their entire lives. Some areas are modern, there are also historical parts with old British colonial architecture, and also neighborhoods which are hard to describe. I can only say that Calcutta has to be experienced – its smells, colors, and crowds. Reading about it does not prepare you for the impact of life there. But Calcutta is a holy city, home to Kali.

I had maintained a Buddhist discipline since my experience in India three years before. Now, as I walked down the streets of Calcutta with RN, the face of Mother Kali would appear to me and that continued for some time. I would be walking, eyes open, yet I was still having these visions of Mother Kali. This startled me and even started to confuse me. As I was trying to be one-pointed in my discipline, not really understanding why it was happening, I continually pushed these visions of Kali away. It would be almost 20 years later before I understood why this was happening to me. Shortly thereafter, RN and the group had to leave to return home. I remained for only a short time after RN and the other two group members had left, and then also returned to Toronto. This trip to India was not nearly as eventful for me as my first trip in 1977.

I didn't stay long in Toronto and went back to India six months later. This time I went to Leh in Ladakh, North India, in the Himalayan mountain range. Ladakh was once part of Tibet, the Guge kingdom. It was annexed by the British in the late nineteen century, becoming part of Kashmir. Recently, in the 70s, Ladakh was opened to foreigners. When I got there in 1981, there were only a few small hotels and guest houses compared to now. During my last visit in 2014 there were so many hotels and guest houses, well over a hundred. Ladakh is still primarily a Buddhist kingdom, with many Tibetan styled temples called 'gompas' strewn throughout the territory. Many of these 'gompas' are still in use today. Some are very large, Hemis gompa being the largest in the territory. The capital of Ladakh is the small mountain city of Leh. Today it is brimming with so many 4X4s and taxis, taking both tourists and trekkers to many destinations in the region. Just 35 km outside of Leh is the highest navigable road in the world, at 18,380ft above sea level, known as Khardungla. You can go there, but it's a restricted area, and its necessary to purchase passes first as the road leads to Pakistan and there are military bases and it's an area of tension.

Namgyal Tsemo Gompa, Leh

(photo by author)

Leh is at 11,500ft above sea level. When I first got there, just to walk a short distance took a lot of effort. I felt out of breath and my body felt heavy, hard to move. After two days I had acclimatized and felt like my old self again. I stayed in a B&B run by a Ladakhi family. There are many temples scattered around Leh, some are quite old, dating back to the 14th century. High above Leh, at the top of one of the jagged, bare rock mountains there, rests Namgyal Tsemo, a small gompa made up of a group of buildings. Tsemo was originally built as a protector temple overlooking the region, and then the Maitreya temple portion was added much later. I decided to climb up to the Maitreya temple early one morning, just as the sun was rising. I felt that I should meditate there and I had found out that it was not open on a regular basis but that a monk was there early in the morning to perform the various rituals which were used to maintain the spiritual forces there. Hiking up the rough, rocky terrain in the cold morning air was refreshing but the thin air made breathing more difficult. I was getting closer to the temple, just passing a small chortem, (Tibetan for stupa) when I became aware of what appeared to be a figure, suspended in the air to my right. This figure wore a simple white turban and was only visible from the waist up. Although I was looking forward as I climbed, I could clearly see this figure at my right as if I was looking right at him. This apparition instructed me to sit on the edge of the chortem, which I did. Just as I sat down, a ferocious demon like creature wielding an axe jumped up out of the chortem and rushed right at me. I could see it, even though it was happening directly behind me. My vision had become forth dimensional! Fear rushed through my entire being like an angry wave. I instantly countered it, visualizing the form of Avalokiteshvara with eleven heads and eight arms and chanted the sacred mantra, "Om Mani Padme Hum", applying the esoteric tune. Miraculously, the Divine form of Avalokiteshvara appeared, going beyond my own visualization, taking on a surreal intensity and closeness as if I was absorbed in the form life of the deity. I was so taken in by the power down pouring from the deity that I lost sight of the demon. Realizing that the demon was gone I stopped chanting. The figure that I had first seen was also gone but a message entered into my consciousness that the test was passed but not 100 percent. Pondering for a moment on the meaning of this message, I realize that I had stopped the meditation too early.

I had missed an opportunity to increase my devotion and connection with Avaloketeshvara. From one of the teaching poems: "Milarepa then replied, "As a rule, all trouble making demons and Devas in the outer world...we accept as helpful conditions and grateful gifts. Like the crack of a horsewhip, these demonic obstacles are very good stimulant for indolent beginners. An unexpected shock will undoubtedly sharpen one's awareness. Also, these demonic obstacles are the very causes that will aid one's body and mind in devotion, and quickening the arising

Samadhi: to those advanced Yogis who have already reached stability on the Path, these obstacles become the nourishment of Wisdom. Such hindrances will also deepen the clarity of the Light-of-Awareness and improve one's inner Samadhi. Through them supreme Bodhi-Mind will arise, thus enabling the yogi to better his devotions in a rapidly progressive way". (17) This statement from one of Jetsun Milarepa's songs, which in fact are very deep teachings, proved to be very true. Many years later, RN and the group made great progress, entering into the deeper esoteric world by battling and overcoming the constant attacks by various types of these demonic forces. Today people do not believe in demons and such as they only exist in stories or movies. Unless you've experienced this, it is very hard to believe. Just before I climbed down the mountain, another message entered my consciousness; I was to go to Varanasi. That's it; I wasn't given any other indication of what I was supposed to do. I felt at a loss and instead of heading up to Tsemo, I headed back down to the B&B. I was not in a great emotional state. I knew I had to obey this order, yet I didn't receive any type of verification. It was given to me and that's it. Thirty-two years would pass before I actually did meditate in the temple at Tsemo. After this unexpected intense occult experience, I spent the next few days sightseeing, as my flight to Delhi was still a few days away. Once I returned to Delhi I took the train to Varanasi.

Varanasi is considered the oldest and holiest city in India. Being a Buddhist, I wondered why I was instructed to visit the center of Hinduism in India. Varanasi was known as Benares in the not too distant past. The Ganges River, the holiest of rivers in the Hindu religion, is the main spiritual focus to the worshippers who visit this holy city. Varanasi is considered the place of Lord Shiva, but many other deities are worshiped there. There are temples strewn throughout the city, many of them are very small, more like places to make offerings of incense, food or prayers. Varanasi has both an old historic area by the Ganges and a newer addition to the city. Several miles outside of Varanasi is a park called Sarnath, where The Lord Buddha Gautama gave his first teachings. The difference in the feelings one experiences between the two locations is very distinct. Sarnath has a permeating feeling of peace, very 2nd Ray. You feel so peaceful, even serene, there. Varanasi, on the other hand, feels more like an agitated, busy and intense atmosphere, everything but calm, more 4th Ray with a strong 6th Ray and 1st Ray sub-ray.

I stayed in the old section of Varanasi in a rundown, second floor hotel, not too far from the Ganges. I had no idea what to expect or to do when I arrived. On the second day that I was there, I was walking peacefully along the banks of the Ganges River, taking in the sights, when I heard a voice within my consciousness directing me to turn right and keep walking. When I got to some stairs the voice told me to go up and I did. When I got to the top of the stairs I continued walking but almost immediately I was standing over this old man, very frail, who seemed to be waiting for death, lying motionless except for his breathing in the hot overhead sun. He must have been roasting away. Right away I knew what I was supposed to do. Pick him up and put him into the shade near a wall, several meters away. This man, like so many elderly, came to Varanasi to die and to have his ashes scattered in the holy Ganges. But I couldn't do it! I couldn't pick him up. I just stood there frozen for a minute. My mind was racing. I turned away and went to ask for help. After several minutes I stopped and asked an Indian man what to do. He just said that the man was dying, what's there to do? My mind was reeling, running wild like raging horses thrashing against each other in a crowded stockade. I felt this huge pressure rising up from me, filling my head, so that I felt top heavy. I turned back to try and help the old man, but someone else had moved him into the shade. I felt terrible, a complete failure, except that I was able to follow and obey psychic instructions to a point. I had no idea why I panicked and was fearful with a task which in appearance should be easy. Now my head felt heavy, thick, and my prana felt so blocked. What was happening to me? I was so ashamed at this failure that I never told anyone about this incident. I was being tested by the Higher Forces and failed them. Deep inside I knew it! How could I redeem myself for this failure? I was just at such a loss, nothing seemed to interest me now. Not much else worthwhile happened in the remainder of this trip and I returned home with a heavy heart.

Little did I know at the time that I was about to enter a very difficult period in my spiritual life that would last for years. It was the beginning of the awakening of the Dweller on the Threshold. Maintaining a concentrated spiritual focus and keeping one foot in the world while working full time makes for an intense and very dynamic life. Returning from India I had to find a place to live, a new job, and re-integrate with the group energy. This did not take me too long to accomplish, but I still felt very unsettled. Before this last trip to India, I had felt in tune with my Essence/ Soul. The Work felt very alive and fresh, and my intuition was bright. Now I felt so different and I couldn't feel my intuition, it was gone or blocked. I was in a dark place. RN also noticed this, and for a while I could not chant with the group. I had a lot of work to do on myself.

Dealing with My Dweller of the Threshold (DOTH)

Sometime in 1982, after returning from India, I started working in the Ontario government as a records manager for the Cabinet Committee of Natural Resources. Actually, first I worked in the Ministry of Education on a contract position a friend got for me. Then, from there I went to Natural Resources. It was not a difficult job and I seemed to have a natural ability to organize information. It's important that whatever job you do does not interfere with your effort in the Work. If your daily job ends up reinforcing the DOTH, then it may be necessary to change jobs. It is important to earn a living and fulfill a purpose in society, but one's job is just that...the Work is one's Life and it must come first in importance. Not to work and rely on others is not an option for the sincere disciple on the Path. The disciple is a responsible citizen who carries their own weight in society. The group is there to help if one of the members runs into difficulties, just like one's family, but is not expected to support a lazy member who feels entitled or thinks they are too advanced to work to earn a living.

I didn't write much about my childhood, as it was basically a very normal kid's life with sports, model aircraft and trying to build stuff. I was an only child and spent a great deal of time alone. Not until I was in my late teens did I realize that my father was very overbearing and too affectionate towards me. I was continually pushing him away as he was hugging and kissing me too much. My mother on the other hand was cold and distant. When I finally left home at 20 I would visit them each weekend for dinner. I remember looking forward to this weekly visit but eventually I noticed that once I was there, my energy level would drop down and I felt a sadness and almost immobile. Later, when I had been in the group for several years,

I still visited my parents regularly on the weekend for a dinner and maybe a movie. RN started to notice the change in me the day after my visit. He could see that my spiritual energy/shakti had been affected in a negative sense, there was a big blockage. Then, one day, he called for me to have a serious talk about my parents. He had seen that in some past life my father and I were lovers. In this life, he incarnated as my father to learn to love in a fatherly, detached way, but his astral body still wanted a more sexual, responsive type of relationship. I didn't want that but until RN enlightened me, I hadn't realized that it was of a sexual nature but on the astral plane. RN said my relationship with my parents was detrimental to my Essence development. He said I had to face my father and tell him the truth, even if he didn't understand, then try to teach him about reincarnation and the soul, to try to transform the relationship.

I had to confront that group of 'I's' that were hypnotized by my father. Standing face to face, I was so nervous. I could feel the fear and anxiety rising, but I focused, and looking straight at him, told him that we were no longer lovers as we had been in a past life and that in this life I was free of him. I remember immediately feeling like something snapped in my head when I said that to him. Later that night, RN confirmed this as he felt on the inner planes that this conscious act had cut through a great deal of the imprisoning astral glamour of the relationship. This was the beginning; there was still a long battle to free myself of my father's influence. I had a lot of difficulty understanding the character traits, that group of 'I's' in me that were the result of being conditioned by my father. My father wasn't the least bit interested in learning about reincarnation or the Soul. My mother sided with my father and they both maintained an arrogant, closed, unloving attitude towards me. Then it dawned on me; they didn't truly love me. I was an extension or projection of their feelings of personal self and that was why they were never happy with my life choices. For instance, when I wanted to become an artist and an art teacher, they were very upset, thinking that it wasn't a worthy career. Eventually I freed myself of this negative relationship to a satisfactory point so that it was not affecting my Essence anymore. Part of this work was to visualize aspects of this relationship, observing the type of emotion it generated and then chanting, placing the visualization in the flame of awareness to further detach and weaken this group of 'I's'. This took several years, but I could actually see and feel the inner change that was taking place. Just to be clear, other group members had healthy relationships with their parents, thus their tests were different and didn't require breaking the association with their parents. In this work, the teacher points out the problem and gives insight into the method to overcome the hindrance, but it is up to the student to do the work. The teacher gives guidance, and, if the teacher is advanced enough, he also can add to your Essence a quota of energy/shakti to help increase your own spiritual vision.

I was sharing an apartment just by High Park with Alice during this difficult and trying time. I was doing a lot of painting as I was finally getting some inspiration. This is when I really started to focus on my painting, creating some occult inspired works. Also at this time, we had a small B group meeting a couple of times a month at our apartment. (Just a quick note, we called it a 'B' group as to differentiate it from the main or original group that RN taught. B groups were taught by other members of the main group under RN's direction.) Ian, a fellow I met in India, came to Canada and was living down the street. He came to the B group, as did Sam, RN's only son from his first marriage. There were a couple of other members in this small group, Heather and Hugh. B groups generally didn't last too long but were primarily a screening method to filter our weaker aspirants, while the stronger, more sincere aspirants would slowly be integrated into the main group. The B group was also a means for the group members to teach and gain further experience. Learning through teaching is an aspect of 'dana paramita', or giving from the Essence or heart. Then they would be introduced to RN and he would determine if he was going to teach them. The main problem with this B group was that Sam, RN's son, wanted to be the teacher. He wanted to show his father that he could be just like him. Unfortunately, he didn't have the occult knowledge, insights, and inner connections that his father had. It was his spiritual personality that wanted to be a recognized teacher and he imagined himself as a great teacher. Of course, RN recognised this and tried to teach his son that one of the first aspects of the occult path is obedience and humility. Sam was not interested and wanted to be the teacher directing all of RN's students. He eventually left the group, even after we all tried our best to help him. In the B group work we did not give out the esoteric mantra, but concentrated on the knowledge aspect and silent meditation, such as the Five Dhyani Buddhas of Transformation.

After the B group had dissolved, I was having so much difficulty with dealing with the effort to detach from the negative controlling influence of my father that RN felt that it would be best if I moved away from Toronto temporarily. This was to create distance on the physical plane, so my Essence could recover and allow me to really analyze the negative aspects of this particular father-son relationship. So I moved to Calgary and sold cars, began painting again, and went hiking in Banff. Living away from the group and being totally on my own was very difficult. I didn't know anyone in Calgary. One day I was meditating by the Bow River and I felt this huge heaviness descend on me and seem to fill my entire head. My head felt like a concrete block. It was like a dull, heavy, throbbing headache but not a headache. My meditation just didn't seem to clear it away. I knew this heaviness represented my failure in Varanasi returning to me. I didn't know it at the time but this was the first part of a very esoteric stage on the path. It was not a fun stage! I would learn later the seriousness of this stage. From time to time, RN would call to see if I was making any progress. I really felt I was in a dark cycle, pedaling uphill against the wind. I lived in Calgary for just one year and then RN felt it was time for me to return to Toronto. I had won a small contest at work which gave me some extra money and I bought a one-way plane ticket and flew home and back to the group.

Group Challenges

Once back, I quickly found an apartment, got a new job as a salesman in the printing trade, and bought a used Toyota Celica. This was a period when the Work as the 'Great sifter' became very active, separating the gold from the sand. Everyone was being tested by having to face, what Gurdjieff called, 'chief feature', which is not really the same as the Dweller on the Threshold but they are connected. Both deal with one's inner weaknesses that act as a major blockage to making spiritual progress. The 'chief feature' is easier to see in a group environment as it's more on the surface and doesn't require the same level of separation. Ellen ran away from the group, moving to India while I was away. That's a whole story in itself. Ellen had a Masters degree in Russian language and literature. She had always been in love with RN. RN enjoyed her company on an intellectual level, but she wanted more, beyond the student-teacher relationship. He had helped her in many ways, both spiritually and in her daily life. He cured her eating disorder and got her to live a healthier lifestyle. She even tried, in a subtle way, to interfere with RN's family life, which was not easy for his wife as she was being tested too. RN had to put Ellen in her place but she couldn't accept just being his student. This seemed to be a recurring theme for her as it turns out, Ellen told me once that she had had affairs with both a high school teacher and a university professor. Her 5th center seemed to enjoy men who had knowledge, power and were teachers. RN was being tested too, as Ellen was a much younger woman than his wife. But RN was an advanced disciple and he was not trapped by his 5th center and the glamour created by it. Ellen left the group, which was very sad as she was a good friend and she did a lot of excellent work for the group. She was instrumental in typing RN's teaching discourses and then editing them, building a collection of esoteric writings for the group. Because of her effort, typing and editing, she gained a great deal of knowledge. RN saw that she had great potential in the Work but unfortunately she surrendered to her weakness in the 5th center. She was not asked to leave the group but instead chose to run away. All of us were being tested as the intensity of the Work forced everyone to face their inner, most hidden, weaknesses.

"Beware lest thou should'st set a foot still soiled upon the ladder's lowest rung. Woe unto him who dares pollute one rung with miry feet. The foul and viscous mud will dry, become tenacious, and then glue his feet unto the spot."(17)

The above quote mirrors what started to happen with all the members in the group as their Dweller on the Threshold began to manifest and show its ugly head. When the DOTH first awakens, the Disciple is generally caught unawares and before they even know it their mechanical, lower impulsive actions prove to be very harmful to both themselves and the group. This is what happened to Ellen and later, while I was living in Calgary, to RN's wife. No one is immune. It is this force of the DOTH that has destroyed many group efforts, even the TS fell under its dark cloud back in the late 1920s with the Krishnamurti incident and the Star of the East.

One day, when RN returned home from work, he found that his wife, Emma, had run away with their daughter, Sally. When RN told me, I was shocked, in disbelief. RN found out later that she had actually found a job and enrolled Sally in a school in British Columbia, Canada. Emma was a very proud 6th Ray personality, with a strong will, and was under the impression that she was always right and didn't like being disagreed with, unwilling to listen to any criticism directed at her, no matter how constructive. She had selective hearing. I used to say that she wore heavy duty earmuffs all the time. This was an aspect of her Dweller on the Threshold. Other than that, she had a strong essence and a very caring nature. She was a true Aquarius and just saw everything with a different logic. RN eventually found her in British Columbia through a private investigator he had hired. When I returned from Calgary, I gave RN some financial help to get Emma and Sally back. This was such a bizarre time for the group! The really strange thing is that while I was in Calgary, I had had a dream of Sally wandering in a city; she was lost and looking for her home. As I said, everyone was being tested as we were about to enter into the next stage of the group work.

So now I was selling printing. I remember that when I was a teenager, I had told myself that I would never end up being a salesman like my father. This must be the mad work of karma! There was a small earth tremor in Toronto that year; I remember my entire bedroom was shaking, waking me up early in the morning. With RN's guidance my spiritual state seemed to be improving and the 'heaviness', which I spoke about before seemed to recede a little. There was no B group now as we had to dissolve it because of Sam, as I mentioned before. The group met at RN's house for regular meetings. RN was concentrating on developing mandalas that expressed the ideas of the work. He would start with a simple pencil drawing. Meditating on the initial idea, he would gain further inspiration and finish the mandala in a simple pen and ink drawing. Then he would have his wife, Emma, enlarge it and paint it in very bright colors. The focus of our study were these inspired diagrams and charts that became meditation tools and greatly helped us to get insights into many difficult esoteric concepts. See example teaching chart below.

Nadine, RN's eldest daughter, had moved from Holland and came to Toronto, she was living with her father's new family. Unlike her brother, she did not express any type of spiritual ambition. She seemed to have a natural understanding of many of the work ideas. Like her father, she was an amazing cook. Not too long after being with the group, she and Edward, the

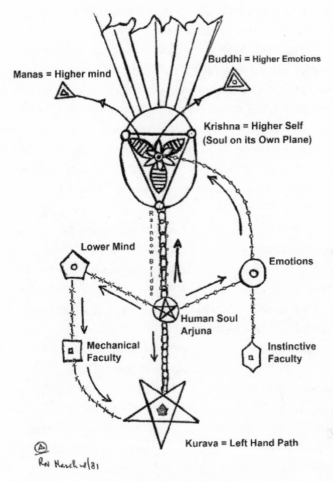

Example teaching chart

lawyer, fell in love and were married. They lived in a big house in High Park, not far from RN's home. Nadine soon gave birth to a son, Martin. The marriage didn't last long and after a little more than a year, Nadine and Martin were living at RN's home. One would think if two people were married in the Work there would be more chance of the marriage working out. This turned out to be a very complicated situation. The marriage didn't break up because of the usual reasons that you see in everyday life. Edward didn't cheat on Nadine, there was no shortage of money, they didn't fight, even after a little incident where Nadine spent over $10K on her visa card in one month and there was really nothing to show for it. That's still a great mystery! No, the marriage broke up because of the awakening of Edward's Dweller on the Threshold. He became absorbed by the DOTH, it turned out that he was a low class black magician for numerous lives from a distant past. His whole being changed and soon he couldn't even go to work anymore. This put some pressure on the group, as several of us had to help him financially for a short time. He became very cold and unfeeling towards his wife and child, plus his DOTH become very poisonous. This is very dangerous and relates to one of the hidden esoteric facts as to why the Master D.K. initially had groups that only communicated by correspondence. When you have an esoteric group that is connected to the Masters, the teacher becomes a focal point of the group energy. He is connected more deeply to the inner ashram. At the same time, all of his close students are connected on the inner plane to him. The DOTH is like a foul smelling swamp full of impurities. If the DOTH gets out of hand, as in Edward's case, then a portion of it transfers to the teacher and then to the ashram. This is very dangerous. Fortunately, Edward had a strong trust in RN's occult abilities and knowledge, and followed instructions to battle his DOTH, and accepted separating from his wife and child. He also realized that if he didn't face this ordeal head on, he could end up as a 'lost soul' or die early. Dealing with Edward's DOTH would turn out to be a long, long, drawn out group effort that lasted for a number of years.

Sometime in the spring of 1983, I moved to San Francisco to start a B group there. RN had an inspiration that San Francisco would be a good city to try and build a second group, since there seemed to be a strong spirituality in that city. Jill was already living there as she had to leave the group for some time, again because of the DOTH, and had moved there. I flew down and she arranged for an apartment close to her in South San Francisco. I found employment selling material handling equipment in San Mateo, a 45 minute drive away. Then I started to search out and visit different spiritual groups. The first group I met there was called 'Light on the Bay'. They studied the works of Alice A. Bailey but they were dominated by a strong guru personality who had very little real knowledge. The group met in Berkeley. I became friends with the lady whose house they used. In a short while, I showed them my knowledge and impressed them and I tried to get people together to start a new group. I was only able to get a few people, and we started having group meetings every couple of weeks. One aspirant who seemed to have a stronger interest was George. We became friends and eventually shared an apartment together in the Sunset district of San Francisco. I visited other groups in the area, but I was disappointed, not finding any other aspirants that were aligned to the esoteric teachings along similar lines of thought as the group in Toronto.

After I had been there for several months, RN came with his wife, Emma, and I arranged a small group retreat just north of the city, at a cottage on the Pacific coast. RN gave a very strong teaching for the two day retreat but not long after his visit this new little group seemed to die. Except for George, I could not find other aspirants who had a strong interest. The group in Berkeley was not ready for deeper teaching, so that relationship ended.

Then RN and the entire Toronto group came for our yearly WESAK retreat. We all drove out to Lake Tahoe, a few hours northeast in the mountains. We rented a beautiful, large, A frame type cottage that could sleep 15 people. The weather was sunny and warm, except one day when it snowed enough to turn everything white, but then the sun came back out the next day and the temperature climbed and the snow melted. We had a full house for WESAK. It was during this WESAK that Edward's DOTH became so strong for RN (I think this is when it entered him) that I had to drive Edward to the airport and get him back to Toronto and away from RN. At the same time, Nadine fell in love with George as her marriage with Edward was in shambles. My DOTH hit me hard during one of the meditations and I was stuck in it. I didn't know why it happened, but I was able to see it happening yet was helpless to stop it. RN was furious with me. I tried to explain what I saw and experienced but he didn't want to hear about it. The energy was very strong that WESAK, affecting many of us in one way or another. Everyone went back to Toronto, except Nadine, who stayed and visited with George. That relationship never really budded. George got cold feet and then one night while I was out, he moved out from the apartment and quite literally disappeared. The attempt to build a group in San Francisco ended in failure and RN felt that I should return to Toronto as soon as possible.

Importance of WESAK

One area of the Group Work that I haven't yet discussed is the importance of WESAK. For the group, WESAK as a point of experience in time acted as our spiritual New Year.

WESAK occurs once a year, during the Full Moon in the sign of Taurus, generally at the end of April or the beginning of May. This is a momentous spiritual event that is little recognized in the West. Even many Buddhist religious groups that celebrate WESAK rarely comprehend the significance of this sacred event for the awakening of the human soul in the hearts of all men and women.

At the exact moment when the Moon is Full in the sign of Taurus, the Buddha Gautama, the Enlightened One, returns to earth in a sacrosanct ceremony that takes place in a sacred valley deep in the Himalayas. This ceremony is officiated by Lord Maitreya, the World Teacher, accompanied by many Masters of Wisdom, Initiates and disciples of various degrees of awakening. (The word 'disciple' in this context doesn't connote a follower, but indicates a degree of Soul evolution.) The Buddha appears briefly over a particular flat rock formation at the center of the valley. Lord Maitreya and the Masters are arranged around this rock in a ritualized pattern and begin to invoke the blessing of the Buddha by chanting the mantra of the Buddha. Surrounding the Masters are the Initiates (Arhats, Lohans, and Maha yogis) while the disciples are positioned on the periphery of this ceremonial event.

The Buddha soon appears, as if descending from heaven, his color is radiant gold, his right hand raised in blessing. His blessing is focused on the Masters of Wisdom who then act as a spiritual transformer, radiating this blessing through the other participants and then out to humanity. On the rock below the Buddha there is a large bowl of water that receives the blessing and is then passed around for all those in attendance to partake of. The ceremony last only a short time. Many who attend do so in their subtle bodies, not always in their physical bodies. Once the ceremony is completed, all the participants return to their fields of service and the valley is once again empty and silent.

Why WESAK is so Important

I'm not really a follower of the Buddha, so why should I come to a WESAK ceremony?

WESAK is not just for Buddhist. It is a sacred, spiritual, not a religious, event for all of humanity. Lord Maitreya, the Initiates and disciples represent the spiritual inner government of humanity which is often referred to as the Spiritual Hierarchy. The Spiritual Hierarchy is concerned with the evolution of the Soul in all mankind. The Hierarchy guides, teaches and uplifts struggling humanity. There are many members, some who appear periodically in their physical vehicles and walk among men. When these great beings appear in physical manifestation, they make a great and lasting impact on Humanity. To name just a few of these world wonder workers: Moses, Hermes Trismegistus, Lao-Tse, Adi Shankara, Zoroaster, The Buddha, Ezekiel, The Christ, Krishna and Plato. The Angels and Archangels and the Devas also make up the Spiritual Hierarchy as they work closely with the Masters and Initiates.

Taking part in a WESAK ceremony puts you in touch with a yearly effort by the Hierarchy. You now share in the Work of the Great Compassion of the Buddha to uplift humanity. You create a Dharma association on the inner planes of Spiritual endeavor with the Schools (Ashrams) of Masters who work unceasingly for humanity. This association is like a seed planted in the fertile soil of Aspiration to Soul awakening, Service to the Schools of the Masters, and service to humanity. The WESAK ceremony not only has a present purpose but it also helps to speed your own spiritual evolution in the future. Taking part in the WESAK ceremony year after year helps build a karmic relationship with the Buddha, (Bodhichitta, awakening to the path of enlightenment) Masters and Initiates of the Spiritual Hierarchy. This relationship is very important because it can guide your future lives and assist with positive rebirths to enable your spiritual growth to continue more rapidly.

In your effort to help the world at this time, there are three things of a practical nature that can be done.

1. The active instruction and mobilizing of the known aspirants and disciples of the world, no matter in what group they work.
2. The call to participate of all who can be reached, advising them of the day of opportunity, mobilizing them for a vast world effort to arouse afresh a spirit of good will, and calling for a united use of the Great Invocation on the day of the WESAK Full Moon.
3. The arranging of public meetings on as large a scale as possible, to be held on the day of the full moon of WESAK. I mean by this that meetings should be held for the public at some time during the eighteen hours which precede and include the time of the WESAK full moon.(18)

What is it that should be accomplished at each momentous WESAK full moon? I shall state the objectives sequentially and in the order of their importance.

1. The releasing of certain energies which can potently affect humanity, and which will, if released, stimulate the spirit of love, brotherhood and of good will on the earth.
2. The fusion of all men of good will in the world into an integrated responsive whole.
3. The invocation and the response of certain great Beings, whose work can and will be possible if the first of the objectives is achieved through the accomplishment of the second objective.
4. The evocation from the inner side of a strenuous and one-

pointed activity on the part of the Hierarchy of Masters, those illumined Minds to Whom has been confided the work of world direction.(19)

The next few months are intended to be (for all disciples in all Ashrams) a period of preparation for fuller service. No cost is too great to pay in order to be of use to the Hierarchy at the time of the WESAK Festival; no price is too high in order to gain the spiritual illumination which can be possible, particularly at this time. (20)

You will note that the Buddha focuses in Himself the down-pouring forces, while the Christ focuses in Himself the out-going demand and the spiritual aspiration of the entire planet. This makes a planetary alignment of great potency. Should the needed work be accomplished at the WESAK Festivals, the needed alignment in the world can be made. (21)

Spiritual workers are needed now, and taking part in a local WESAK Festival unites spiritual workers around the world to help build this most important planetary alignment which helps to construct the 'rainbow bridge' (antakarana) between the Hierarchy of Enlightened Minds and Humanity. This is more than wish fulfillment, it is an ideal that we can all strive for making a strong effort to be part of this world spiritual event. The 'forces of light' wait patiently to be called into activity on earth by the aspirations of a united spiritual invocation by a waiting humanity. First meditate on the importance of the WESAK Festival, and then ask yourselves from your 'inner-most-self', do I truly want to serve on the 'upward lighted way' for the benefit of mankind. (22)

Our group occult calendar revolved around the Full Moon cycles and the year ended and started with WESAK. During the first ten years of the group, from our first WESAK to the tenth one, we managed to do short, intense meditation retreats over the WESAK period. A Full Moon period covers the day before and after, plus the actual Full Moon day. For our WESAK retreats we would arrive two days before the actual day of WESAK, one day to prepare and then start the retreat one day before WESAK. These retreats were very disciplined with a strong 7th Ray format, there would be no talking during the actual three day full moon period, with four daily meditation periods, silent study, group study where RN would lead, and pure vegetarian meals. All questions were in writing and RN would read them and then discuss. If any member had some sort of spiritual or occult experiences during meditation, then they would write a detailed description and pass it to RN who would later comment on it. If it was a worthwhile experience, he might discuss it with the whole group. On the day after the WESAK three day period, before we headed home, we'd break our silence and have a big vegetarian feast. Most members of the group found that the WESAK experience was a catalyst for their spiritual efforts for the coming year.

I will just mention a couple of the WESAK retreats, describing events that seemed to stand out from my own perspective and experience.

The first WESAK retreat (1975) was in a wooded area where we had rented a large cottage in Sutton Quebec. Both the Toronto and Montreal groups attended, so we had at least 20 attendees. It was a beautiful place but there was one big problem, there was only one bathroom for all of us in the cottage. This meant a long line-up in the morning! You could not complain either as there was no talking allowed. The cottage came complete with an equipped kitchen and we would set up a buffet styled eating experience. Fortunately for us, RN was an excellent cook and he loved to cook! He had his cooking helpers and they would prepare everything, chopping vegetables, arranging the spices and making sure all the pots and fry pans were clean and ready. RN brought along his personal wok from home. Most of our meals were a cross between Chinese and Indonesian stir-fry with delicious jasmine scented rice. Watching RN cook was an experience in itself, as he stood by the wok shouting orders for this spice or that sauce. He never used recipes. He cooked with his intuition, guided by a very heighted sense of smell. His food was always very tasty and each meal was different. I never tired of his cooking.

The first meditation session was early in the morning. We sat on the floor in two concentric circles, back to back. In the center of the circle was a simple makeshift altar with a white, unscented candle and incense. We used sandalwood incense as the Master D.K. mentions in *Treatise on White Magic*, somewhere in rule #10, that sandalwood is a 1st Ray incense that helps break up negative vibrations and thought forms in the location where it is being burnt. The group has used sandalwood incense ever since. RN would lead the meditation; we did both chanting and silent focusing on the golden flame in the lotus of the heart. We chanted the mantra of Lord Gautama, the Buddha, the fully Enlightened One. (see mantra below)

"Om Namo Tasse Bhugavato Arrahato Summa Sum Buddha sa".

RN would calculate the exact time of the Full Moon, the point of the actual time of WESAK and we would meditate at that exact time, chanting the mantra of Lord Gautama, the Buddha. Sometimes the exact time of the Full Moon ended up being in the middle of the night.

The meditation periods were generally just over an hour in length. We worked hard on centering our focus on the golden flame in the heart. This would help quiet the inner talking and prepare us for chanting with a strong inner focus. Then we'd visualize the Buddha, Lord Gautama, above our heads, radiant gold in color, with his right arm raised in blessing and we would start chanting the mantra of the Buddha, four times aloud and then four times silently, which would equal one round. There are numerous tunes available to chant this mantra. What is most important is to visualize the Buddha clearly and to chant with a deep reverent feeling. You should feel as if you are making an offering or dedication to the Dharma as you chant. It's important that you do not chant mechanically, losing focus and just chanting with your mouth. The mind is focused through both the effort to maintain the visualization and the thought of offering. With this type of effort one then attains what the Tibetan Master D.K. calls 'alignment'. When everyone in the group is doing this with sincerity, then it's the group effort that invokes a response from the higher forces.

During the actual WESAK meditation, many of the group members had some type of experience that they wrote down for RN to examine and discuss. I had an intense experience, which was my first experience of Samadhi; I was focusing and visualizing the flame, but it turned into a radiant golden sun and as my focus became more intense, I seemed to move closer and closer to it. This created a great deal of tension, not on the physical body, but in the psychic totality , or chitakasha. It felt like my astral body was vibrating and shaking. The tension reached a very high intensity, my focus was like a drill. The sun became like living fire, then, there are really no words, but I blasted through this sun as a point of conscious, feeling identity, with purpose. On the other side was a radiant golden world of light, with liquid golden Beings that shone like stars. The feeling was of quietude yet I was just this point of awareness, moving rapidly towards another sun in this world of brilliant light. One of these beings seemed to be watching and directing me. What I remember is that this golden Being had very powerful eyes. In the space I was in, there was a sky and sun and I was told telepathically to focus on this sun, too. My total feeling was of self moving rapidly through space. There was no sense or feeling of my body. I was not in my astral body, this was not astral travel. As I focused on the second sun, I rapidly soared nearer to it and again a feeling of tension began to rise between me and this sun. Then I passed through this sun also and came into another world. This world was a vivid multi-colored canvas, and I was flying as a point of conscious awareness over a jungle with a glowing, golden-white pyramid in the distance that rose above the jungle greenery. I started to move towards it rapidly but I was stopped, somehow I couldn't go further and in a second I felt myself flow back through the top of my head, back into my body. To me this was a remarkable, wonderful experience. RN agreed and in fact was quite surprised. I remember him saying that it usually takes many years of mediation before achieving this feeling of integration and Samadhi.

Learning From an Occult Experience

What did I learn from this experience? If an experience is real, not just an astral vision, then this happening becomes part of you, you can always feel it, even years later, plus there must be something you can learn from it. What I learned, for me, was very profound. In Raja Yoga, as you concentrate on a form (rupa) a relationship exists between you and

(1)   the seer, the one who creates the image or visualization
(2)   the object that is seen, what you visualize
(3)   the act of seeing – seeing is an action

In fact, this relationship exists in everything, in all life experience; it's just that we flow through life unconscious of this fact. In Yoga you intensify this relationship through meditation and make it more conscious. When your concentration becomes more one-pointed, the distance between you, the seer, and the object of meditation is shortened. This creates a point of tension, which increases as this distance becomes less and less. When there is nothing but your own feeling of concentration and the object of concentration, in Raja Yoga, you've reach dharana, or true concentration in the yogic sense. Next, when you become one with, or enter into the object of meditation, this is dhyana, real meditation, and then a state of Samadhi ensues, which is usually translated as a higher trance state. This is incorrect, as this state is not a trance, but the English language is limited in such descriptions. As you become one with the object of meditation, you pass through a laya point, which is like a force field that separates the lower and higher worlds. This is explained in the *Yoga Sutras of Patanjali* which is the work book for the serious student of Yoga. The other thing that I realized is that after such an experience, though the flavor of the experience may remain with you for a day or so, the fact is that you come down, back to your normal day-to-day world. You are not some special spiritual being just because you had a cool experience. Until you've crystallized in your Essential Self, such experiences are generally the result of past merit on the path in another life and are not indicative that you are some great advanced soul.

Years later I met and also read about some individuals who had strong spiritual experiences, too, except they believed that they were enlightened. Soon they were able to convince others that they were an enlightened being, here to change the world. In a short time they formed large organizations and a philosophy based on their experience. Such groups relied heavily on the personality worship of the leader, not on any true spiritual tradition. They were far from enlightened and in many cases they ended up living like kings, but in time, eventually, some scandal would result. Many of these so-called 'enlightened' teachers were good writers and knew how to say the right things, which to the general spiritual seeker would seem like words of wisdom. When assessing a teacher, it's necessary to look beyond their words, look at their actions. Do they conform to the tradition of the great teachers of old? But this is another area of discussion that I will pick up later.

At another WESAK the group rented a reconditioned farm, where the barn had been transformed into a retreat center. The old barn stalls were now bedrooms, very simple but comfortable. We enjoyed this location and actually had two WESAKS there. This was Anna's Farm, located just a few miles north of the city. We followed the same format as the previous year with our meditations. This year, though, the exact time of WESAK was in the middle of the night. Getting up at 4 a.m. to meditate took some effort for some of us, since we had meditated at midnight and then would also meditate again at 8 a.m. to continue the flow of the WESAK energy.

One strange incident that occurred during one of the meditation sessions was that a big, black horsefly entered the meditation circle, buzzing around us annoyingly. RN said this fly was sent to interfere and disturb the group harmony. As we chanted, the fly, like a bullet, was driven into the flame and with a loud 'pop' disappeared. We were amazed at this incident because at that time we didn't understand the possibility of negative influences like a Dugpa, a dark force, trying to interrupt us. That was the only negative influence during that entire retreat. Although the meditations are extremely important during a WESAK retreat, we also spent a lot of time in group study. RN taught through diagrams that would express the teaching. He had various diagrams that were painted by his wife – of the Tao, Astrology, Buddha Dharma, 4th Way, and Yoga Vidya. The diagram below teaches about Chitta Vritti and the Three Gunas that I talked about before in the chapter on Yoga.

Vrittis of the Mind
Designed by RN

RN would explain them but we had to visualize these charts instead of taking any notes while he explained it. If you take notes you're actually focusing on your note taking, just movement center, not on what's being said. If you visualize, then the teaching goes more to your Essence and feeds your higher nature. During the meditation at the exact time of WESAK most of us felt this deep peace descend as the visualization of the Buddha became very clear, almost real in its radiant golden form. Just a note, this feeling of peace is actually a vibration, very subtle but deeply penetrating, helping to purify and energize our entire spiritual being. I noticed that when our WESAK meditations were intense this same feeling would be present at our WESAK meditation each year. It was a very distinctive feeling.

For another WESAK we rented a Boy Scout camp on the Niagara Escarpment, a very scenic wooded area with individual cabins and an amazing kitchen with the dining area filled with picnic tables. For this WESAK event we had some guests from the USA, along with the regular group, making around 20 people taking part. To add to the 7th Ray aspect of this event, we had Zen styled blue-grey robes made. We would only wear the robes for the WESAK retreats and when we sat down to meditate. This time we all sat in one large circle during meditations. During one meditation, I was allowed to see that there was a cone of light enclosing the group. It was wider at the bottom and tapered as you went upwards, but I could only see that it went up into more light. We were meditating on Avalokiteshvara, even though this was the year before we received the blessing of the Master R who charged the mantra with his energy/shakti. Still, when there are 20 people chanting together four times a day, a dynamic energy is created that seemed to build each day.

During one of the meditations, the deity Avalokiteshvara manifested in a vision, in its blazing, flaming form of the eleven headed, eight armed rupa, to myself, RN, and his wife. The three of us saw the same vision. It was so real, ablaze with Divine energy/shakti, that I can still get a picture of it today, many years after the actual experience. RN felt this vision was significant because the three of us saw it and that it indicated the inner connection with not only Avalokiteshvara but also with the occult school or ashram of the Masters. It was not long after this that RN received the blessing of the word of power from the Master R. The intensity of the meditation periods caused many of us to take naps in the late morning and the afternoon in order to have the strength to keep going. With long meditations your legs begin to ache from sitting cross-legged for so long many times a day. Near the end of the retreat it was necessary to learn how to detach from the leg and knee pain so it wouldn't interfere with concentration. Again, many of us felt that 'presence' and peace during the actual WESAK meditation. You almost felt like you were there, in that sacred valley in the Himalayas.

When you do group work and begin to invoke higher energies, the Essence has to become the 'Holy Grail', like a sacred chalice to (1) catch the blood of Christ, (2) to hold and maintain this blood and (3) to increase the amount held. What does this mean? The idea of the 'Holy Grail' is figurative and meant to describe an esoteric fact in the science of meditation. The 'blood of Christ' is the Divine shakti/energy that descends from the higher planes, via the Soul on its own higher mental plane. This energy/ shakti is invoked through chanting a sacred mantra, especially when it's done in a group. The Christ here does not refer to Jesus Christ. The Christ in the esoteric teaching represents the Divine Mediator, who connects the Divine Supernal, the life of the Logos, with his creation. The Divine Shakti is the Flame of the Logos that is invoked by a group effort. It has to be absorbed by each member's Essence and then safely maintained and not leaked out. This is a very esoteric point. It is hard to build up and maintain this Divine Shakti but it's very easy to leak it out. Giving into negative emotions such as anger, jealousy and arrogance will immediately cause this Shakti to leak out. The problem though is that this Shakti has to go someplace. If it flows into the matter aspect, then the Lunar Pitris, the aspect which represents the aspirants' weaknesses, the DOTH and the negative aspects which lay dormant in the aspirant can be charged with energy/ shakti instead of allowing the Essence to absorb and hold it. Consequently, the matter aspect, the lunar pitris, grows stronger at the expense of the Essence. Unfortunately this happens much too often during the final stages of the Probationary Path.

A Pitfall on the Path

Many times sincere aspirants to the sacred Wisdom have very good, heightened experiences caused through a temporary alignment with their Soul on its own plane, but because the shakti/energy is so much higher than they are used to, they cannot hold it in their Essence which is just beginning to awaken, then this energy flows in and blows up the DOTH like a balloon which becomes huge. They are completely unaware that this is happening. The problem here is that since the Essence is still not really awakened or stable and has not separated from the ˒ personality, the aspirant's Dweller (DOTH) is also awakening which can result in an occult or spiritual personality being created which gives the impression that they are totally awakened, if not enlightened: in touch with higher forces or even God. This is all an unconscious, un-awakened reaction, except the aspirant thinks that they are conscious and awake. That's the danger! Unfortunately what generally results is some form of paranoia or over-stimulation of the passions occurs and the organization that was initially built up with the best intentions falls apart, causing disillusionment and spiritual confusion among the followers. The Master D.K. termed such false teachers as "Busiris, deluders of Souls". From the *Labors of Hercules*, "His is the work to bring delusion to the sons of men through words of seeming wisdom. He claims to know the truth and with quickness they believe. He speaks fair words saying: "I am the teacher. To me is given knowledge of the truth and sacrifice for me. Accept the way of life through me. I know, but no one else. My truth is right. All other truth is wrong and false. Hark to my words stay with me and be saved."(23)

In such cases, the focus is on the personality of the teacher or guru not on the teaching itself. This is so common. This is very prevalent in the West. Even with the Tibetan Lamas, who are quite genuine, their followers are always more focused on this Lama or that Lama and the teaching they give out sounds nice but has little substance. The Tibetan Lamas work hard to uphold their religious traditions, they are compassionate and want to share some small part of it with us in the West. So many western adherents of Tibetan Buddhism are under the mistaken impression that these Tibetan Lamas are awakened or even enlightened. In fact, only a very small handful of them have real knowledge and are awakened. Only a handful of them actually meditate.

So how did RN and the group avoid this pitfall? RN never made any claims and always taught that it was the esoteric teaching that was important, not the personality of the teacher. Our group was eclectic, studying so many different philosophies, both Eastern and Western. RN wanted us to awaken and develop our own 'vivkea' or spiritual discrimination. He even recommended that we visit other groups and teachers to see what we could learn. Although RN was the teacher, he always used various occult books as references. When RN taught, he was always referencing different teachings of the Ageless Wisdom. Thus all of his students had fairly large libraries of spiritual books. Once you have a certain degree of knowledge, it is much easier to see through others whose knowledge is false and not get caught by their sweet sounding phrases.

We did, however, focus a great deal of time studying Theosophical teachings, which for us included the works of the Master D.K. through the works of Alice A. Bailey. RN admitted that he had learned a great deal through the books published by Alice Bailey of the Tibetan's teaching but also from the 4th Way and Yoga Vidya. No one teaching has the perfect system or 'has it all', but if you study several teachings and look for the common thread that ties them together, then you can get a more complete picture. This is why I could never understand those individuals that only held to one book, whether the Bible, Torah or even the Secret Doctrine of H.P. Blavatsky. To me, they saw the Divine work through horse blinkers, thinking they had the complete picture.

Three of us Take a Trip

One year, during the late spring, I, with Samantha and Jill took a trip through New York State, visiting many groups, ashrams and temples. We met Philip Kapleau at the Zen Center in Rochester. He had written a couple of worthwhile books on the Path of Zen. The Zen Center was very well known in Zen circles. We had an interesting conversation with him and were able to converse about both Zen and Yoga. We actually surprised him with our explanation of the five categories of modifications of the mind. He knew of them, but not in the context of actually being able to observe them in others. Next we visited a Japanese Zen temple which was identical to its sister temple in Japan. This temple Dai Bosatsu was so beautiful, located in the Catskills, you could feel the serenity even before you entered in. The temple took us back in time, from the austere yet refined silent beauty of the meditation room with heavy wooden architecture, to eating a small but very tasty vegetarian meal in silence with the monks. Next we visited a very large Chinese Buddhist temple complex which was completely empty except for one Taiwanese monk. He told us that it gets very busy on weekends, when the Chinese community from New York City comes up. We took a tour of the main temple which was just the opposite from the austere environs of the Japanese Zen temple. This Chinese temple was filled with statues, carvings and pictures depicting various aspects of Buddhism. There was an amazing, tall, wooden statue of Avalokiteshvara with eleven heads, eight arms, and a thousand arms carved out of wood, it was at least fifteen feet high. Later we had some tea and a short discussion with the Chinese monk. He asked us what we liked about the temple and what area of Buddhism we were studying. We told him we were meditating on the form and attributes of Avalokiteshvara. Then he asked us a question that I've never forgotten and it took me several years to answer. He asked, "If Avalokiteshvara, who has eleven heads, eight arms, a thousand arms with a thousand hands and on each hand there is an eye, which is the right eye?" This is a type of 'koan', an unanswerable question that in fact does have an answer which can only be arrived at through contemplation. The intellect by itself will never get it!

Later we went to a New Age Zen temple, Zen Mountain Monastery, that had been built in a converted church. It didn't have that austere feeling that the Japanese temple did, even though the meditation room was a big empty room. Unfortunately, most of the people were out and there were only a couple of people to talk to. While we were conversing, I had a strong impression that all these temples that were springing up in North America had a much different purpose than people would generally think. All the Hindu, Buddhist, Jain, Taoist, and Zen temples were like shafts of Spiritual Light which helped to puncture holes in the thick materiality thought-forms which are so strong they are almost strangling real spirituality in North America. They create a balance, otherwise the power and glamour of matter would have too great a hold on society. The final temple we visited before heading home was a Tibetan temple called Karma Triyana Dharmachakra, the present North American seat of the Gyalwa Karmapa. At that time, the temple was an old resort house built in the 1930s or earlier, in the hills above Woodstock NY. I would return there many years later, when they had built a larger traditional styled Tibetan temple. We returned home with many stories to tell and wondering why temples like the ones we visited in the US weren't being established in and around Toronto.

Love and Sex

During the late 70s and into the 80s, there were many types of spiritual groups active all over North America. Interest was budding in Tibetan Buddhism as the Dalai Lama's peace initiative towards China was making him very popular. Also, there were many so called, "enlightened gurus" who claimed to be custodians of the Way. The New Age of Spiritual liberation had really begun as traditional religions started to lose some of their following. With all these different groups, congregations and ashrams, there soon emerged stories about sexual escapades and abuses within them. Many times these stories were about the leader or guru and involvements with their disciples. Our group also went through a period of sexual awakening, experimentation and discovery. Sex is the hardest subject to broach for most people because of the negative thought-forms regarding all aspects of sex created by the Judeo-Christian religious traditions. Though there is a lot of literature on sex from a psychological point of view, from Freud on to the present, there is almost nothing in esoteric literature. Yoga talks about transforming the sex drive from the lower chakra, svadistana, sacral chakra to the higher chakra, throat chakra or vishuda. The Tibetan Master D.K. in *Treatise on Cosmic Fire* talks about the evolution of the sexual passions that will in time be transformed as humanity evolves in the distant future: "On the astral plane, the home of the desires, originate those feelings which we call personal love; in the lowest type of human being this shows itself as animal passion; as evolution proceeds it shows itself as a gradual expansion of the love faculty, passing through the stages of love of mate, love of family, love of surrounding associates, to love of one's entire environment; patriotism gives place later to love of humanity, often humanity as exemplified in one of the Great Ones".(24)

For most of us the idea of making love means having sex.

Love and sex are almost interchangeable words for many. Love is a great mystery for just about everyone. There are no courses that really discuss love, yet the word love is used constantly in so many different contexts. In Sanskrit the idea of love can have six different words and meanings to express this emotion.

1. Prema, affection, love relations between couples
2. Maitri, to sacrifice for another or others, act of unselfish love
3. Karuna, radiant compassion, love for the few who need help
4. Mudita, sympathy, gratitude, an expression of love for one or many
5. Upeksha, dispassion, equanimity, love of ALL
6. Bhakti, devotion, surrender, love of deity, love of God

In Mahayana Buddhism, the Path of the Bodhisattva is the path of love on a divine level, comprising compassion (karuna), gratitude (mudita) and sacrifice (maîtri). These high ideals are rarely thought about when we speak of love in today's society. The Bodhisattva, in the true sense of the meaning, is a very advanced spiritual Being who through love (Upeksha) makes that utmost sacrifice by turning back from entering the peace and bliss of Nirvana to help struggling humanity. Love is not passive, not just a word to be used lightly by a disciple. For the disciple, intelligent action based on soul or intuitive direction becomes Love-Wisdom.

Love is a word used as often as the word God, with very little understanding of either meaning. In Hollywood, famous couples marry claiming that their bonding is the love of their life, only to split up weeks later citing irreconcilable differences. So love and sex are very complex issues which are at the core of human psychological existence. For the aspirant to the Divine Mysteries these two issues have to become more clearly defined within one's total understanding of self.

From the esoteric viewpoint, a sex relationship becomes the door for past latent karmas to enter. Also from an esoteric philosophical point of view, sex is the lowest manifestation of the desire to unite with the Divine. Sex is an act of uniting, becoming for a moment, at-one with the other; it's an inner unconscious desire for 'at-one-ment'. Man/woman is asleep to the forces of Nature that are all around us. These forces of Nature are likened to a dance or play (Sanskrit – lila) that keeps all life in motion as an expression of the One Life and Light, fulfilling some mysterious Divine Purpose with all existence. Thus the 'Mysteries' were created to help man awaken to these hidden, occult, esoteric truths that hide within the labyrinth of the forces of Nature. Sex and love is at the root of this entire matter. G. I. Gurdjeiff had an insightful understanding of this matter but there is very little in the teaching of the 4th Way on this subject. RN admired Gurdjeiff, as I mentioned earlier but he also felt that Gurdjeiff wasn't kosher, sort of grey, in between white and black. Gurdjeiff was an awakened teacher with real knowledge of the workings of Maya or Vidya Maya as it is called in the Sanatana Dharma. The 4th Way teaches us that man is a machine, and like a machine, in order to understand how it works it is necessary to be able to take it apart and examine each piece and then reassemble it. The 4th Way deconstructs human psychology into five active centers which are further divided into three sections. The five centers are

1) Intellectual center
2) Emotional center
3) Moving center
4) Instinctive center
5) Sex center

Each center is divided into three

1) Formatory (mechanical)
2) Emotional (essence)
3) Intellectual (conscious)

Each of these centers has particular characteristics and functions. The trick to understanding them is to be able to observe them in action with an impersonal eye. This is very difficult. This is where the group work becomes interesting. It is the teacher's skill, along with group reinforcement, which helps to clear the fog that prevents the struggling student from being able to see the working of their psychological characteristics clearly. RN developed a diagram to help us picture the relationship of the centers to Essence (see diagram). This is the practical work, the work of self-discovery.

Now back to sex. Looking at the diagram, the sex center is placed directly in line with the 'sushumma', which is represented by the central channel from the Soul on its own plane, the higher mental plane, down to the physical world, ending at the sex center, (sometimes called the mysterious 5th center).

To understand further and to see how important the sex center is, it is necessary to realize that man, though he may feel as 'one' being is in fact, not 'ONE'. We are a multiplicity. Each center is made up of groups of 'I's', or transient, moving feelings of self as 'I'. The feeling of our self when we say 'I' is an illusion. This feeling of our unity is an illusion. This is our sleep. To illustrate: walking down the street we experience the smell of a BBQ, inwardly you may say, 'I feel hungry'. You say this as if your entire being is hungry...instead it's an 'I' in instinctive center responding to the BBQ smell. Then you notice a billboard advertisement, either a feeling of like or dislike quickly flows through your consciousness, whether you like or dislike it, this is a different 'I' in emotional center. Then you stop and read a newspaper article of interest to you, another 'I' likes it and a different 'I' of intellectual center interprets it. Then as you walk

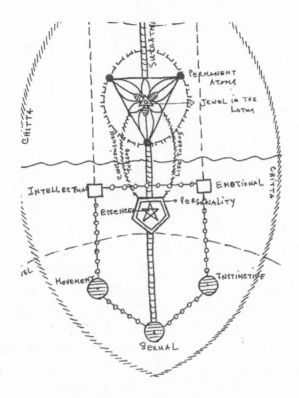

Soul the Personality and Five Centers

along and a pretty girl in a red dress catches your eye, this is an 'I' from sex center.

These different 'I's' are in constant movement and at varying speeds. The sex center is the fastest. With each "I" we identify with creating the feeling, as if our whole being is this "I". We are not conscious of this rapidly changing psychology of 'I's' that occurs second by second, because we are not awake and haven't been educated about our inner psychological, mechanical, flowing constitution. Self-observation is the Work technology to increase and deepen awareness of these different groups of 'I's' and how the centers function. This is the real Work of awakening. Few people, even aspirants, are prepared or open for this degree of introspection. Why? We have a subconscious formulated ingrained idea of who we are. We are comfortable with this inner sleep; the blankets of illusion are warm and cozy. We are under the illusion that we know ourselves. We don't want to shake the tree; it's enjoyable to live in the shade where we are comfortable. The Work calls this identification. This means we are glued to this bundle or group of 'I's' which makes up our personality.

The sex center is the hardest center to see and then separate from. The sex center is the epicenter of our personality. It controls how we look, how we see ourselves, how we think others see us, plus what type of partner we want, what they should look like, what their personality should be like, along with relations with just about everyone else we know. It is a fascinating and complex labyrinth of desires, and I don't just mean related to the physical aspect of sex. Jealousy, envy, gossip and anger that grow from these desires are also groups of 'I's' which live in the sex center. The sex center is so powerful that it pollutes the other centers. For instance, if an individual is unhappy in a relationship, then the sex center will even infect the emotional center, making the individual very negative or even depressed. The emotional part of the sex center is also termed the 'heart of the sex center'. When you say you love someone then you are giving to that other individual your heart, but it's not the heart of your being as most people believe, instead it's the heart of the sex center. The heart of the sex center is the emotional aspect of the sex center. Aspirants and non-aspirants, when confronted with this new information, generally immediately feel that it doesn't apply to them and just ignore it. Piercing the mysteries of the sex center leads to the Esoteric Path and to initiation. Because when you're capable of seeing the truth about yourself, then you begin to break away from the controlling big 'I's' of this center, beginning to separate from personality.

Today many people are interested in Tantra, as they've read that it is a method to enhance their physical sexual experience with their partner. This is totally a distorted aspect of what the real Tantra is. The statues of both the male and female deities locked in what appears to be an erotic embrace are symbolic of bringing polar opposite forces, male/female, duality, into ONENESS. These figures are generally central in a Mandala depicting a strict esoteric yoga discipline, involving extensive visualization, mantra recital, and meditation. Such Tantra disciplines are to transform the sex center and the energy generated by this center to a higher level. There are aspects in Tantra that do involve actual sex, but it is only for very advanced yogis. Jetsun Milarepa, an 11th century accomplished Tantra ascetic, mentions when teaching his disciples that having a partner for the 'secret act' is not something just based on desire and has to be done at the correct time in order for it to be effectual. You have to be achieving a certain degree of pratyahara or inner-centering during the sex act, a degree of detachment, then you begin to transform this activity. There are other stories of men being able to control their ejaculations, but these refer to the physical aspect of the sex center and movement center. It is much more complex than what's told in these stories.

In the group we referred to the sex center as the '5th center'. This 5th center works with types. Many times an individual may picture what they feel is an ideal vision of beauty of who they want to be with. Yet for reasons unknown to them, they never seem to match up with this ideal. There are two reasons that help to explain this and they are interdependent. One is karma and the other is body types. Karma is all powerful and is involved in every aspect of one's life, especially the 5th center. Then there is a silent, instinctive intelligence of the body itself that attracts other bodies based on an unconscious body blueprint. Karma, that force which connects and acts as the glue, helps to fit the jigsaw puzzle together. This is the physical aspect, and then there is the emotional aspect of the 5th center. Emotional attraction is different but there must also be a degree of physical attraction for it to work. Since male and females are polar opposites, generally the emotional part of the 5th center attracts opposites in the emotional sense. For instance, an introverted personality will more often than not find themselves with an extrovert. It is part of a little known fact that all relationships are based on the theory that one partner is the cat and the other is the mouse. Today psychologist look at this as a dominant personality and the weaker personality. But this type of polarity can change over time and circumstance.

One of our group members worked as a hair stylist in a high-end salon. She was an excellent stylist and had numerous local television personalities as her clients. People who work in salons are generally going to have very active 5th centers, as did Samantha in our group. There is one thing to look presentable at the work place but these salons are just vanity factories. Thus Samantha was very up in her clothing styles and her hair changed color or shape almost weekly. She was a divorced single mom with a young daughter in primary school. Her 5th center was very active, not only in her hunt for a new mate but in her dress and mannerisms. Samantha was an example of a disciple caught between two poles; on one side she meditated twice daily, studied, served the group effort, and on the other side was this vivacious, outgoing woman who wanted at all costs to get remarried. When she did get married again, a couple of more times, it was always to the wrong man. Thus, her spiritual progress was hindered because she had to leave the group for short periods following her 5th center dreams. This is an example of the force of one center having such a strong impact on the personality that it becomes difficult for the disciple to make progress. Fortunately, she had excellent guidance, her Essence was strong enough and she persevered on the Path through all these trials, thus her Essence eventually made good progress. At this time in the group history our investigation of the 5th center was our central discussion point and the escapades of Samantha became a central study.

The question might be asked, why are some individuals 5th centers so active and others not? Through the group work, we discovered that it has to do with the center itself, plus past life experiences. Centers, in general, can be of two types; clean and unclean. What does unclean mean? It means that the past life history of an individual who took part in various activities: forms of black magic or sex ritual, has caused an 'extra ingredient' to be absorbed into the center. This extra life force, an elemental, through the law of karma returns to the individual from life to life, or in a particular life again, depending on one's spiritual evolution. Thus, the center has an extra quality, strength, activity and a desire-life. You see this in many celebrities. Do you think Elvis Presley was so successful just because of his looks and voice? He had a very powerful extra something, like an apsara, (feminine entity which adds an attractive element) connected to his 5th center that permeated every part of his personality. We called this, having an 'extra' or a 'K-d' or kama-deva. These extra ingredients are another type of life form called by various names, depending on their particular characteristic. In the occult, these life forms are usually called elementals 'bhutas' in India or (lower) Devas. In general, individuals who have a K-d in their 5th center attract many partners and they seem to move from one to the next, having a restlessness that doesn't allow them to rest. They are generally very attractive and successful, but rarely happy. Another example: the list would be endless but I'm just writing about a couple to give the gist of this knowledge. There are men who in appearance dress well, appear to have normal, productive lives but when they get close to women, the woman finds them creepy, offensive or odious. Why? Such poor souls have a very dirty 'old man' elemental. They are unaware of it and cannot understand why they turn women off so easily. But this is an esoteric fact, it is not general knowledge. The elemental takes over when they are close to a woman and without them realizing it they are leering at the woman in such a way that she feels uncomfortable and is totally turned off. There can also be the reverse effect, which is seen in individuals who lead very quiet lives, unable to mix easily in society, especially with the opposite sex. Some elemental is damming up the natural flow of prana in the 5th center, thus their feeling of 'I-ness' is trapped, they can't radiate to others. They feel fearful, anxious and uncomfortable when they have to interact with the opposite sex. Sometimes they become nuns or monks. This is karma handing out difficult cards to deal with.

A big problem occurs when individuals, like the clergy, try to be celibate with zero understanding of the powers and needs of the 5th center. Energy is neutral and is conditioned by the quality of the vehicle or form it uses. Electrical energy passing through a light bulb gives light, passing through an electric chair results in electrocution. The electricity is the same; the difference is the vehicle, in this case the center. If the center has some type of elemental attached to it, then the energy will be distorted or aggravated and cause a further distortion in behavior. If the priests were allowed to marry, then the 5th center would have a natural, socially acceptable outlet, the energy would be circulated correctly, instead of finding such unlawful means of expression as we've seen too often.

This brings up the topic of centers polluting other centers. The centers are made of ethereal substance finer than any gas. They are invisible to the naked eye, as are the chakras, nadis, and meridians. Each center is a bundle of 'I's' that make up behavioral patterns, a vortex of force that is in constant movement. These centers work together; it is their combined activity that results in the creation of a personality, and yet each center has an apparent independent activity and purpose.

For example, if a young man is waiting for his girlfriend to show up at a meeting place, he can become very anxious, impatient and even agitated, pacing, looking around, even feeling that she may not show up. It is the 5th center that feels anxious but it pollutes both the movement center, making that center more agitated, and adds a negative quality to the emotional center, making this individual feel worried, insecure, and impatient. Also, because of the state of the 5th center in this application, the individual may find that they cannot think rationally. Thus the 5th center has totally disrupted the equipoise of the individual in this situation. The 5th center has power; it affects both thoughts and feelings. It also needs food or stimulation. So if you cut off having sex, as in the case of the clergy who become celibate, it can erupt, driving the individual to unnatural sex acts, depending on the latent past-life sub-conscious tendencies (Sanskrit, samskara) which condition the subtle substance of the sex center or it can become violent or criminal. The Master D.K. hints at this in his writing regarding the substance of sub-plane matter conditioned by the lunar pitris. Many of the problems of the clergy in the past years would have been avoided if they were married. A yogi can becomes celibate when a very advance stage has been achieved. After the 4th Initiation the human soul is transformed on to the Buddhic plane and the need for sex disappears since the aspect of duality is naught. Before that time an aspirant may undergo periods of celibacy but it should only be for a designated period, on retreats or doing some special disciplines. If you have some knowledge and understanding of the workings of the 5th center, its tastes, likes and dislikes, it is much better as you'll have some idea of the type of forces you are dealing with and can observe then.

Many individuals have difficulty reaching orgasm because, unknown to them, there is some entity, generally an elemental, which is attached to the 5th center. Unconscious of this cause, people turn to different means of stimulation in order to feel or get really aroused, such as S&M, bondage and various role playing. This can occur very easily through drugs or heavy alcohol usage or as a carryover from past life experiences. Such elementals, in fact, condition an individual's behavior as soon as they are even in the proximity of the opposite sex. For instance, in the group, one of our members, Jack, was a very handsome young man who women found very attractive. He had that clean cut, easy going look about him. He could find dates very easily but he would only go out with a woman a couple of times, for a dinner or show, returning home early and then end it. Eventually RN approached him about this and he confessed he was terrified of having sex because of his penile dysfunction. He was attracted to woman and wanted to get married and have children, but as soon as he got intimate with a woman he would go cold and would feel very unsettled. This is the effect of a very strong elemental in his 5th center. If he was at work or with friends, he was the nicest, warmest, very helpful individual but once a woman began to show real interest in him, this elemental would take over and he became cold and distant. This is an extreme case. The power of this elemental was so strong that once RN began a program to help rid him of this, Jack ran away and we never saw him again. Because of the power of the 5th center, very few individuals want to face it and deal with it because it is the core of their personality.

An acute example of the power of the 5th center occurred when a young, oriental fellow, Albert, who was excellent in Tai Chi, fell in love with Samantha. He was not Samantha's type as he was short and not that attractive, plus he was considerably younger than her. She also liked men with power and position, much later she married a Japanese corporate VP and lived in a penthouse which she enjoyed decorating. Albert and Samantha got together for just a very short time, but when Samantha withdrew, poor Albert was so distraught that he couldn't remember his Tai Chi moves; in fact he couldn't do anything at all for several weeks. His entire feeling of self had been absorbed by the glamour of having a relationship with Samantha, who, for him, was like winning a lottery and being with a Playboy centerfold. He had become the 5th center! Then when it all crashed his 5th center was devastated; the personality was like in a waking coma, unable to function. It took RN several weeks to help Albert get back on his feet. He was just a probationer in the group Work but after this incident, he left the group and moved to the other side of the country. The light of the mirror of truth was too bright for Albert.

Another member, Frank, was a young VP for an advertising agency and he came to the group through Samantha, the hair stylist, and they soon became an item. They went out for quite some time and Samantha was definitely ready to settle down and hope for marriage. Frank also had an elemental in his 5th center, but a different type than Jack. He liked to keep woman hanging, he couldn't make a commitment. He confessed that he had done this with many women. RN gave him a special discipline so he could truly face the force of the center, learn to observe the thoughts and feelings it created and then counter it. But it was very powerful and one night we found him rolling on the floor yelling like he was in pain, but it was the elemental force causing this. This elemental, as all elementals, didn't want to be made visible. Once it was seen, then the process of detaching from it and overcoming it was possible. These two cases are extraordinary examples but they give some indication of the power of the centers when they have an elemental attached to them. The same applies to the instinctive and movement centers. An elemental in the instinctive center generally results in some type of addiction. In the movement center the results can be various ailments related to motion. The list goes on and on. Through esoteric knowledge elementals can eventually be dissolved or pushed out, depending on one's karma. This world and knowledge of the effects of elemental substance connected with the centers is hidden from humanity. It is not something that you can easily believe in. I've just given a little glimpse into that world. If psychologists had any idea about this, then the entire method of treatment and healing would change and become truly occult methods of healing, which the Master D.K. mentions for the distant future. Such healing is accomplished primarily though sound and color. It is one of the reasons that purity is so important on the Path of Initiation.

Modern psychology does not see the human psyche in the same light as the esoteric science of the centers. You cannot just understand these centers. They have to be observed, studied and meditated on so they are seen through the radiant light of the Soul. The 5th center is the most difficult center to comprehend as it's the fastest center, it pollutes all the other centers and the focus of an individuals' personality is centered there. That's one of the reasons Gurdjieff said that humanity is asleep and everything, all social life involves sex, even going to church on Sundays.

The 5th center is responsible for much of the difficulties in the world today and, of course, in the past. For instance, tyrants have very powerful 5th centers; their feeling of **I**, of power, stems from there, their paranoia, and their need for cruelty and of course their thirst for sex. The intellectual center rationalizes their behavior; the emotional center is frozen, totally polluted by the 5th center, the center in charge. In a very esoteric sense, tyrants are more the manifestation of some Asuras, a non-human, highly intelligent life-form in the subtle worlds that many times can incarnate as a human. A very interesting point is that *if* the emotional center is operating correctly and a person can truly feel, then they cannot consciously do physical harm to another. When a person can feel deeply, then their conscience is active. The conscience is the first voice of the soul that **KNOWS** immediately what is right from wrong.

Schools

Throughout the world there are different schools of spiritual development that lead to the Path of Initiation. The Trans-Himalayan Arhat School is the one that is most active in Western Europe and North America. It was this school that was the force behind the Theosophical Society (TS) which began in 1875. The TS at one time had spread around the world and was very active until the 1930s. There is a lot of literature on the history and personalities of the TS so I will not follow along that route. Instead, what has to be appreciated and valued as a legacy from the TS is the publishing and dissemination of esoteric knowledge through the many books, plus the interest in the hidden wisdom of the east that it created. One aspect of the work of the TS was to transform the ancient Hindu and Buddhist esoteric traditions, Sanatana Dharma, to make it more accessible to the western mind. This meant almost eliminating the Sanskrit rituals and rites. In fact, Theosophy is a blend of Mahayana and Vajrayana Buddhism and Vishista Dwaita Vedanta Hindu teachings. The teaching stresses the importance of knowledge and service to humanity, basically the path of the Bodisattva. After the TS came the Arcane School and Lucis Trust which focused on the teaching of the Master D.K. via Alice A. Bailey. From both of these organizations, many smaller offshoot groups and organizations sprang up all over the world. The teachings were in essence still Theosophy but adjusted for the different time period and with more practical applications added to the pure knowledge aspect.

Another school that is active in North America stems from the work of Paramahansa Yogananda, who was sent to North America by his guru Sri Yukteswar. Both were members of an ancient North Indian school of Kriya Yoga headed by a mysterious master of Yoga, Babji. Yogananda gave out hints as to the deeper esoteric teachings of India but for the general North

American aspirant his teaching was more eclectic, designed to show how all religions have the same uplifting purpose for humanity as a whole.

There are schools in India, for instance, which are very esoteric and have no particular interest in North America and whose purpose is very different. One such school is a South Indian school centered on the sacred hill called Arunachala. Sri Ramana Maharishi was the last adept in residence there. Such schools have a very esoteric purpose, not connected to world service as is the case with the Trans-Himalayan school, but more with the maintaining of the school itself, on the inner planes, and probably with the deeper realms of India as a custodian of esoteric knowledge. These are very deep mysteries.

Related to the Trans-Himalayan Arhat School is the ancient School of Luxor in Egypt. Several adepts from this school have been active in the west, such as the Master Serapis and the Master Hilarion. Mable Collins, an occult writer from the 1860s through to the early part of the next century, was an adept of this school. Her most well-read book is, *Light on the Path*, which is really for advanced disciples, yet it can be read by anyone, it's very cryptic and its poetic quality creates an uplifting, positive vibration. *When the Sun Moves Northward* is another profound esoteric book that combines and blends the teachings of both east and west. It introduces us to the concept of yearly festivals and ceremonies that occur on the inner planes, the ethereal realms, as she calls them, that occur when the sun travels on its northern path. Mable Collins wrote many esoteric books and stories, very slim volumes in most cases, as compared to Helena P.Blavatsky's large tomes, but she is hardly known today.

There are western occult schools such as the Rosicrucian and Kabala, which seemed to have started in Northern Europe and the Middle East. I believe these schools were also influenced by the Trans-Himalayan Arhat School.

The most important aspect of a true occult school is the 'guru parampara' or as it's known in the west 'the golden chain of Hermes'. In Tibetan and Zen Buddhism, they talk about the lineage which relates to this 'guru parampara'. The esoteric aspect of this has to do with the flow of Divine Shakti from the hierophant, the head of the school, down through the different gurus or Masters of Wisdom to the disciples and aspirants that belong to the school. This flow of shakti is conditioned by law and cannot be misused. It is this shakti that unites the school with the purpose, plan, and activity of the hierophant. This chain of shakti is like a ladder that is the path and draws all those who make the correct efforts up the ladder of initiation. To become a member of a school, an aspirant has to have karma with some advanced member of the school. This is the most important point that is rarely mentioned. You may be an advanced soul making progress on your own, but if there isn't any karma with some esoteric school then there will be no connection with one. An aspirant may not be that advanced but if the karma is there, then a connection will occur when the time is right. Gurdjieff called this 'magnetic center'. That brings up another point; when the time is right, whether you're ready or not, a test will present itself in a natural way that is in fact the door to enter into the outer court of an esoteric school. The Tibetan Master D.K. uses the term 'probationary path' to explain the idea of the outer court of an esoteric school. As a probationer, you're being watched from afar by a member of the school. This is another very important point. Most of us assume that our spiritual level is much higher or evolved than it really is. A new member entering into the outer court of a school brings a new vibration into the school aura. This vibration is as yet not in harmony with that of the school. That's why the new member is tested and kept in the outer court as a probationer, so the new vibration does not disrupt the harmony of the school. One way to look at it is that the school is protected by a wall of high vibration or the note of the school. This wall keeps out undesirable elements that could attack or upset an aspect of the harmony of the school. Each new member is a liability. That's why there are many tests of the threshold that a probationer has to undergo to purify themselves, thus becoming slowly in harmony with the school. These tests will happen naturally or may be generated by the school, depending on the level of the probationer. If a probationer fails to purify and transform their negative vibration, they can be pushed out of the outer court until another opportunity occurs and they are brought back into the aura of the school again. This can be in some future life, not necessarily in this life. To be in the outer court generally means the probationer has passed or is in the process of passing the first Initiation. When entering into the next court, the aspirant has become 'strotapatti' or 'stream enterer', having passed the Second Initiation. They have awakened that reflection of the Soul on its own plane, the soul in incarnation, the Essential Nature within and crystallized or stabilized their feeling of a soul there. Such a one can now transfer their consciousness from the personality to this Essential Nature to a certain degree at will and can feel the difference between the two. This is a very important point. The aspirant now begins really to understand the process of liberation, purification of the bodies, alignment with higher forces and initiation as an actual fact. They also awaken to the world of inner contacts and know what 'Left Hand Path' means. They start to learn secrets that cannot be told straight out through the written word. They can still easily fall from this point and be pushed out of the inner ashram, thus discipline and vigilance must be never ending, it actually increases, at least until they've achieved the initiation of the Arhat which is still far away.

There is an interesting esoteric law, an unwritten law, that says that an awakened soul can always see those who are not awakened, no matter what they may say or claim. Also they can see clearly the glamour's that an individual is ensnared in. Unless they have a direct dharma connection, an awakened teacher will not discuss anything that they may see on a psychic or soul level with an outsider. This is governed by Occult Law. This is when the new initiate undergoes suffering. They are still living and working in the world of men but live a secret, silent, occult life that is very hard to share. The awakened one see these New Agers with their 'laws of attraction' talk and discussions of the bliss of enlightenment and talking to higher beings or God as fantasies far from what really is, but also with a knowledge that sees that at least their soul is stirring and starting to impress the personality intermittently. Such an occultist, even at this junior level, stands alone yet with humility and compassion looking for ways to help his brothers in their search for knowledge and happiness.

An Ordeal

"This ordeal must be endured: it may come at the first step of the perilous ladder which leads to the path of life: it may not come until the last. But, O disciple, remember that it has to be endured, and fasten the energies of your soul upon the task. Live neither in the present nor the future, but in the eternal." (25)

In our group most of the members had passed the 1st initiation and were working towards the 2nd and 3rd initiation. The group had become an outer manifestation of one of the ashrams on the inner planes. It was hard to interpret what level RN was at, but near the end of his life he had begun to exhibit 'siddhis' or occult powers. If he hadn't passed the 3rd initiation, he was then very close in my estimation. How can you tell if one has passed the 1st initiation? In one sense it has to do with the level of commitment and determination. The other aspect that is important to consider is that no matter what, the Work comes first. Many aspirants to esoteric knowledge fall to the wayside as soon as they come face to face with those hindrances that force them to confront their own negative personality weaknesses, to see their own ugliness, and then stand firm in the Work in order to transform the lower vibration. We are not talking about petty idiosyncrasies but to use a Gurdjeiff term, the 'chief feature'. This 'chief feature', is comprised of a constant, recurring negative personality characteristic that works so that attention is always focused on oneself.

To give an example, one of the group members, Edward, was a high priced lawyer, generous with his money, polite, and very knowledgeable. Other group members at one time thought of him as too perfect. He didn't seem to get angry, jealous, or talk down to others who were less educated than he was. Through Edward we learned about another unwritten occult law which we've now seen played out numerous times and is very esoteric.

When the group energy increases dramatically through inner plane contacts, it squeezes out unresolved personality issues that must be purified before the aspirant is allowed to move forward. You have the feeling that you've been blessed with the light of insight and esoteric understanding, then everything goes dark.

"Strive with thy thoughts unclean before they overpower thee. Use them as they will thee, for if thou sparest them and they take root and grow, know well, these thoughts will over-power and kill thee. Beware, Disciple, suffer not, e'en though it be their shadow, to approach. For it will grow, increase in size and power, and then the thing of darkness will absorb thy being before thou hast well realized the black foul monster's presence." (26)

You're in a dark, deep pit and you cannot even look up to see that there is a sky above you. Your world has been turned upside down. This happened to Edward. The high group energy brought to light and manifestation that Edward was in past lives a black magician but of a low caliber, more like a shaman, this aspect took over his normal, good personality. His face changed, he even looked different. This was not a case of possession in the horror story sense. There were layers of entities in him that had to be drawn out and dissolved. When I say in him, what I mean is that they were attached to his kama-rupa, the astral body. This could only be done through a Group effort. RN spent hours chanting with the group to break down these 'extras' that were coming out of Edward. Sometimes these extras, as we called them, took the shape of skulls, insects and even lizards. At one point RN was so connected with Edward he knew exactly his mental state, no matter where he was. Many times, at night, Edward would be attacked by forces from the past that would immediately be deflected to RN. Night-time was the worst time for RN as sometimes the attacks were non-stop. To help, RN asked me to stay with Edward at night to keep him awake and conscious, thus reducing the attacks. I would come home from work and take a good nap after dinner and awake just after midnight. Then I would drive over to Edward's place and usually stay to 4 a.m. Then I would go home and sleep for a couple of hours, wake up and meditate and go to work. This went on for almost four years, until Edward was getting strong enough and his kama-rupa had been mostly cleaned out and he wasn't constantly blacking out. It took years of effort, pain and sacrifice for this to be broken down so the light of his soul could again shine through. One thing about Edward was that he recognized his situation and held fast through his ordeal. The Master D.K. mentions, "...the fire at the heart of the group life is becoming more and more vital, and consequently more and more *spiritually* destructive". (27)

Edward was an extreme case. It happened to others but not to such a degree. But this is the only case where the disciple's mind was blended into RN's mind. But those who did not run away, and there were quite a few who did, showed that their Soul's were committed to this Work and the school. Thus they had passed the 1st initiation and were in the process of effort for the 2nd initiation. This process is sometimes hinted at in old occult books as passing through the 'ordeal'. It is an ordeal! No doubt about it! Edward became a group work in himself. RN made great progress and developed mantra powers through this period, as he was constantly chanting the esoteric mantra, sometimes with the group and also alone. It was an ordeal for the three of us, more so for RN and Edward, thus we all made strong progress and merit by helping Edward. It took about nine years. Four of which were very intense. The Master D.K. talks about this, "The initiatory process between the first and the second initiation is for many the worst time of distress, difficulty, realization of problems and the constant effort to "clear himself"(as it is occultly called) to which the disciple is at any time subjected. The phrase stating that the objective of the initiate is "to clear himself" is perhaps the most arresting and illuminating of all possible definitions of the task to be undertaken. The storm aroused by his emotional nature, the dark clouds and mists in which he constantly walks and which he has created throughout the entire cycle of incarnated living, have all to be cleared away in order that the initiate can say that – for him – the astral plane no longer exists, and that all that remains of that ancient and potent aspect of his being is aspiration, a sensitive response to all forms of divine life and a form through which the lowest aspect of divine love, goodwill, can flow without impediment." (28)

Mantra

The occult clearing process was done through the magical power of mantra. At the beginning of the book I mentioned that the group had received a 'word of power' from the Master R. Over time this mantra had become more powerful, especially in group efforts. Through the group chanting to help clear Edward, the power of the mantra increased dramatically. By the end of this one, long process, RN began to achieve 'mantra shakti'. What this means is that if a disciple chanted with RN, the chanting would have immediate effects on the disciple's state of being. RN said that as his knowledge of mantra increased, he learned to use a mantra like a sword to do occult operations. Just like a surgeon can cut out a tumor, the real occult teacher can use the power of mantra to cut out impurities in one's astral body. Thus as the group became 'clearer', the power of the group invocation became stronger. The door to another world was about to open.

Mantra is the most sacred science. Though the words of many mantras are known, the secret lies in the transmission of the mantra. Without the correct transmission a mantra is almost useless, maybe five percent effective. The transmission of a mantra involves several aspects

1) Correct wording,
2) Correct note or tune,
3) Correct rhythm or meter,
4) How to chant or where to place, focus, the mantra,
5) Correct visualization, the form it takes, in most cases the deity involved.
6) Some understanding of the meaning of the mantra.

A mantra is the sound body of a deity. This is a very esoteric statement. A deity like White Tara has its form or 'rupa'. This is its physical body. The mantra for the White Tara is its true name and sound body. Mantra cannot be taken lightly. Mantra is like an esoteric communication device. Just like when you use a push button phone, each number has a note designated by a beep. Hitting a certain number of a series of numbers creates a pattern of sounds. If you've keyed in the correct pattern of numbers, then you will shortly be connected to another person whose contact number corresponds to those numbers that were typed in on the phone. Thus the use of a mantra is to contact or invoke a deity that corresponds to a particular mantra. If you key in the wrong numbers when you try to reach someone, then the tune of beeps is incorrect and the connection with the person you wish to speak to fails. It's the same with chanting a mantra. If everything is not applied correctly then you will not invoke the deity. Just like having a land line when the phone installer connects your home line with the system, a mantra has to be connected to the deity by someone who has the ability to make the connection and make the mantra active. For our group it was the Master R. This is the real meaning of lineage or receiving the transmission or the whispered teaching. (More on mantra in Part II, Practice Section)

In Tibetan Buddhism, the lama or a group of lamas will achieve a contact through a ceremonial invocation that they call an empowerment. Generally the empowerment is to a deity or a Mandala of a particular Tantra, such as Chakrasamvara. Once you've received the empowerment initiation, you are taught to follow a complex series of visualizations to build up the power of the form that you have been initiated into. But they do not give you directions on how to chant the mantra. Generally they tell you that you can chant in any way. The true key is not given. It is my feeling that many of the Tibetan lamas only know the ceremony as they have been taught it. The group chanting that they have memorized does at times invoke the presence of the deity. I've experienced this at several empowerments. When I asked for more directions after the initiation rite, as to which in a series of mantras the key mantra was and how to chant it with the correct note, the Rimpoche or officiating lama said it didn't matter. Though I find the Tibetan lamas that I have had the pleasure to meet very sincere to a point, I feel they do not believe that we in the occident, or non-Orientals, are capable of the strong discipline that is required to understand the sacred teaching, thus they only give out portions of the teaching and in such a way as to keep a student busy with non-essentials, yet maintaining the Tibetan traditions. Another aspect is that it is only a few advanced lamas or geshes who have achieved some understanding. The average lama doesn't even meditate and they are not, as so many believe, enlightened.

The study and practice of mantra requires the 5th and 7th Rays. The 7th Ray is very important. Ceremonial order or the correct type of ritual is the means by which an individual or group invokes the higher energies. To many, the idea of an altar and offerings belongs to another age. An altar with the appropriate statue or 'rupa' acts as a focal point for the down pour of energy. Once the altar is established then the order of offerings, both mental and physical, is very important. A question you can ask yourself is, "which is most important, the Master or the deity?" It is the Master who facilitates the connection with a deity. So the offering first is to a Master. Tibetan Buddhists and Hindus both follow this order, but one may find their ceremonial offerings very long and overly ornate and what I call 'flowery'. This is where the old traditions run head on into the new, trimmed down form of old traditions. What is important is quality of the offering, and that the offering of obeisance comes from one's conscious effort to be in Essence. This is where deep feeling is important. The feelings of humility, surrender, and devotion are of utmost importance.

The 5th Ray is like spiritual engineering, there is an exactness that's very important. The correct order must be maintained and the visualizations and chanting have to be precise. As one makes progress, this precision just becomes part of you. This is the science of Yoga.

From the Master D.K. on the group work: "The group must focus the energy at the very center of the group being; the group must carry the force from point to point and from veil to veil; the group must project the destroying energy and become ultimately aware of what each veil hides; the group must perform the activities (seven in all) of purification; the group must meet, accept and distribute the descending spiritual energy which will finally consummate the work done. The group – through the use of that descending current – will drive the forces of evil back on to the astral plane and will together work with the three aspects of the first ray. These are typified by the Voice, the O.M. and the Sound.

"In the above you have in reality a great formula for group activity and also a potent method (once the group can unitedly work together) for the cleansing and the re-organization of the forces active in the world today." (29)

The above instructions on the group work by the Master D.K. are very precise, 5th Ray, and only for advanced groups. This entire quote is pointing to the importance of mantra as a means to invoke higher energies and this instruction also hides, between the lines, the understanding of the use of mantra in alignment with a group focused on a deity. When a group can wield a mantra effectively, the group will come under attack by strong forces of resistance that will try to stop the group work. The Master D.K. in Letters on Occult Meditation writes about the dark forces and the "brothers of the shadows", or Left Hand Path. These forces exist but not like they are shown in the movies today. If you read such Indian classics as the Ramayana it gives an account of the different forces yogis have to contend with. Jetsun Milarepa in the stories in the book One_Hundred Thousand Songs of Milarepa sings about the non-men that he has to tame that have attacked him on the inner plane. My teacher RN experienced this also and the group helped him with group chanting. By defeating these types of attack, the yogi can make great progress. Jetsun Milarepa mentions this fact in a couple of his songs. The group must be able to use the 1st Ray aspect of mantra to destroy these forces. This helps in a very esoteric aspect of service, the breaking down of old thought-forms that these forces embody that imprison the social fabric of our society. This is the deeper aspect of group work and that is why meditation is so important.

Today, what I call New Agers don't like to use the word 'evil'. There is this holistic approach that we are all ONE. In the absolute sense, yes, but not in the day-to-day reality. Our world is based on duality, hot-cold, love-hate, war-peace, day-night and good and evil. We all pray for peace and equality but unfortunately, especially in the Kali Yuga, or 'dark cycle', it is a noble aspiration, not a true possibility. Lao Tse explained this to Confucius in the famous story of their meeting, where Lao Tse showed him the disparities in nature, how nature is a constant struggle, a foreshadowing of Darwin's theory of the 'survival of the fittest'. In Buddhism, samsara or 'worldly existence' only ends when you achieve Nirvana, other than that samsara, using a 4th Way teaching, results in the idea of *eternal recurrence*. Life with all of its problems, entanglements, enjoyments and ups and downs never really changes, only in appearance. Today technology has enabled greater opportunities for a more educated world, greater comfort and leisure in one's physical life, but has our emotional life changed? Have we overcome greed, jealousy, anger, arrogance, or hate? The world appears to have changed on the surface but underneath it is the same.

Some Thoughts on Astral Attacks

One problem is that our modern, techno-literate western society is generally so well educated, individuals believe that what they read is what they know. They mistake the word for the reality. "I know it, I've read all about it" is too often the response they give. This is just one example of the 'mind is the slayer of the real'. It's a subtle type of arrogance. Evil exists in the totality of the ALL. It is the force of resistance. The force of resistance acts as a thrust block to push evolution onward. Evil exists on the inner planes of existence as it does on the physical plane. It is the yogis' service to combat evil to aid the forces of evolution. These forces keep man asleep. Evil is inertia, the path of least resistance. When man begins to awaken, to become Man #4, it is necessary to counter the path of least resistance and venture on to the Path of intense self-discovery, no matter the costs.

Many members of the group have experienced different types of astral attacks. Attacks can take on many forms and they do not just happen during a meditation period. A probationer who is entering the door of discipleship is very prone to attacks during the hours of sleep. Until you've reached an advanced level, most aspirants are not conscious during their dreams. Dreams may be remembered upon awakening but to actively react during a dream is difficult. Another period when an attack can occur is during the period between waking and sleep. For instance, just as you're falling asleep you feel and hear a loud buzzing sound. The first instinct is to move, you try to move your arms but you can't, it's as if your body is frozen. This generally creates a fear sensation and the mind begins to race. Then you feel as if the body is beginning to rise up, levitate and then spin uncontrollably in the air. This can cause more fear and even panic. You feel totally disorientated. What's happening?

In the above example, the individual who was experiencing

this had their consciousness pulled into their astral body. They had separated from the physical body, thus they could not move. It is the astral body that is floating upwards and creating the sensation of spinning, yet it feels like you are still in your physical body. The attack is two pronged. 1) Moving the aspirant into their astral body and 2) Creating the feeling of fear and helplessness.

This is not done to take possession of you but to steal the group 'shakti' that has been built up in the Essence through the group work. The group shakti is exceptional! It's like special, high octane fuel verses regular fuel. When the group energy/ shakti is stolen like this, the disciple is left empty, plus the negative forces in the disciple immediately take over and the Essence is knocked out because all their fuel is gone. It can take weeks to get back up, depending on the strength of the group and the teacher's abilities. The negative force that is attacking gains strength from the group energy/shakti that it takes into itself.

What do you do when you're being attacked? In the above situation, as soon as you realize that you are shifting out of your physical body and that this is an attack...instantly focus on A) your Master or B) your patron Buddha (deity) and chant, visualizing either A or B. When you visualize either A or B, make sure the visualization is alive, with the form radiating flames of power that fill your entire being. Visualize with power like you are holding a flame thrower, you are in a battle. Continue chanting until you feel yourself back in the physical body and can move again and then spend another five minutes or so centering. If you still feel awkward, get up and have something sweet to eat. This will anchor you back into the physical body. The big thing is to conquer the feeling of fear and helplessness that is pushing on you. Persevere in your chanting as this is a battle; focus on the visualization and the chanting. Do not allow any other thoughts or feelings to enter.

Being attacked in your dream is much harder to counter, unless you can awake in the dream and chant. Any type of situation where you are being attacked by an assailant with a sharp implement like a knife or axe can be dangerous if they actually cut you in the dream and you bleed. Another type is if an animal, like a snake or insect bites you in the dream. I've seen actual puncture marks left on a disciple from the dream. Such attacks indicate an astral vampire is trying to steal your Essence energy/shakti, that special soul energy which has been built up and held in your Essence from chanting and meditating. This is very bad! Not only can they steal and drain your Essence energy/shakti they can leave a poison in your system. This can even lead to sickness, unless your teacher is capable of recharging your Essence with soul shakti and absorbing the poison into his body where he can burn it. When you awake on the astral plane during the attack, chant. Do not try to fight the attacker in hand-to-hand combat. It can work but it is not as effective.

Another type of common attack is through the 5th center. It can happen in the period between waking and sleep or in a dream. This is when the physical part of the 5th center is aroused by the power of an apsara, maybe taking the form of a very attractive woman and causing the 5th center to ejaculate. Then the sex shakti goes on to the astral plane and is absorbed by the attacking entity. Again, this will drain your Essence shakti and leave it empty and very weak. In this case, not only do you have to chant but also to pull the feeling of ejaculation back to relax the erection. Of course this type of attack is more common to males but woman can also feel like they are going to climax and they have to counter it in the same manner.

External attacks can be of many types, coming from a host of different entities that try to project fear in order to shake your meditation. This is very similar to a dream attack where they want to steal the Essence shakti that you've built up during meditation. If in a past life you were involved in doing any type of black magic, blood sacrifices, or involved in sex rituals, the material residue in your astral body can attract elements connected to some of these past lives that can hold you back in your spiritual progress in this life. A connection to a school on the 'left-hand path' (vama-marga) from a former life becomes a huge blockage to overcome. Such schools do not easily let go of their old members. Read, *The Blossom and the Fruit* by Mabel Collins, a true story of a black magician. In this story Fleta aspires to enter the White Brotherhood and through karma she has met her master but because of her dark past she must undergo many tests to uplift her soul into the Light. It's a marvelous story, not easy to believe unless you have the eyes that can see. The ending of the book is a real soul opener. It shows one of the powers of a great Master affecting the destiny of governments and nations.

On a more basic level some of the common attacks can be along these lines. As your meditation improves, you might feel at some point that you are not alone in the room; maybe if you have sight, you see all of a sudden numerous pairs of eyes peering out of the darkness, just staring at you. This can definitely create an eerie cold feeling. Notice if the room becomes cold, if so, it's an indication that the visitors are not friendly, time to visualize and chant. If the eyes are just staring, then they've just come to see what is causing a change in the astral (a disturbance in the force).

Another situation is that as you are meditating you become aware that there is some force trying to enter, a window begins to crack and break open astrally as this force pushes towards you. This is occurring on the astral plane, the window is not really breaking. This is the beginning of an attack. You still can push it back out as it is just at the point of entering.

Attacks from groups of entities and elementals generally only occur if one is very advanced or there is a strong left hand path connection. Jetsun Milarepa underwent such experiences and his uplifting songs, which are in fact his teachings, outline numerous examples where he battled groups of non-human entities. The great Indian classic, the *Ramayana* is another example where Lord Rama, with the help of Lord Hanuman, defeats hordes of demonic elemental non-human entities. Unless you've experienced something like this, it is very hard to believe these stories which are taken as myths and old folklore tales.

The group underwent years of attacks, primarily from two individuals who had been connected to left hand path schools in some past life. The teacher then becomes the focal point and takes most of the brunt of the attack. In some cases, when the group is chanting together to break the attack, some of the poison may also filter through to some of the individuals in the group. Then the teacher, again, has to pull it out of the students and dissolve this negative substance. This is a very difficult time for the group but more so for the teacher. The group becomes magnetic and each member is responsible for staying centered and focused as much as possible. If a group member lets their attention slide in a negative direction, they could let down the group defensive wall and the resulting attack through them can hurt or overload the teacher, who is already dealing with so much. For the uninitiated this is a bizarre reality and not easy to believe. I've never been able to find any type of information on this aspect of the Work in any occult books.

Mantra and Deity

A mantra and a deity are ONE and the same. A deity is a crystallized immortal, an individualized identity existing in the Logoic etheric body. A deity was man in past kalpas beyond measure. There are thousands of deities, some are closer to humanity and thus easier to contact, while others are far, far away. A deity represents or expresses some aspect of Logic law. "Real laws are beings who by interaction create certain definitized manifestations which we are able to see, One can align oneself with one such law and by doing so one can work for a being who directs a part of the Work." (30) This explains the deeper meaning of the term 'patron Buddha' or 'Yidam'. If the Logos were a diamond, the deities are the many facets in that diamond. A deity acts as the Divine Mediator between the One Supreme and the many in creation. The rupa or form of a deity is not arbitrary, it is based on certain principles which capture the meaning and characteristics of a deity. A true 'bhakta' is one who has a devotional relationship with a deity. For the occultist this means that you are conscious of and abide by the laws of that deity. If the relationship is superficial or imaginary, then the rules do not apply. For instance, if you're a devotee of Mother Kali, you must be a strict vegetarian. If you break the rules then the deity withdraws until the devotee again wins the favor of the deity and communication and blessings are restored. This is sometimes called the 'mystical marriage', and like in a real marriage, you have to be true in your devotion to the deity. You can't fool the deity. Buddhist deities being more 2nd Ray, more radiant with the power to save, seem to be less restrictive than Hindu deities.

One of the main importance's of having a relationship with a deity is that it gives you the opportunity to give up or surrender your different 'I's' to the deity. Gurdjeiff understood these concepts but spoke of them in a more emblematic way, "one must study these beings and learn how to become useful to one of them". (31) This is the deeper knowledge of Gurdjieff which Ouspensky never understood. Gurdjieff called this *'obligation in the Work'*. He pointed out that obligation and responsibility are two different things. One has responsibility to one's family but obligation is only to the Work. When you really understand it, then you will know that the Work is like a jealous mistress.

Meditation using symbols or watching the breath are very good disciplines but can only take you so far, because, underlying subconsciously, there is the thought that it is your effort, you have control; you can do it yourself and become enlightened. On the other hand, surrendering to a deity helps to weaken the grip of the personality on the soul. By kneeling down you are lifted up. The 'grace waves' from the deity help to melt down the negative substance of the personality and in time transform not only the substance but even the old behavioral thought patterns.

The personality covers, hides and limits the soul's expression in the three worlds. Surrendering weakens the personality 'I's' and eventually leads to the way of renunciation, the path of no-thought. Surrendering has to be real, deep and from Essence, otherwise it's just your lips moving. Then the vitality of the personality is replaced by the energy of the deity. "The Self of Matter and the Self of Spirit can never meet. One of the twain must disappear; there is no place for both." (32) Through the years of intense 'sadhana' and yogic discipline, one's entire being, mind, body, and prana are transformed and purified.

Faith, knowledge, and discipline,
These three are the Life Tree of Mind.
Non-attachment, non-clinging, and non-blindness,
These three are the shields of the Mind. (33)

This doesn't just happen by sitting back and praying or

imagining. A Herculean effort is required that tasks the limits of the aspirant's entire being. Remember, though, that there is an occult law that the aspirant on the Path is *never given or undergoes any test or ordeal that is beyond the aspirant's capabilities*. You may feel like you're a hair's breadth away from losing it but in many cases tests are designed that way, also testing your perseverance and will.

Although the group initially chanted the mantra of Lord Shiva, I don't feel we, as a group, really created a relationship on the inner planes with Lord Shiva. Next the group focused on Avalokiteshvara, (Chenriseg) with eleven heads and eight arms, as our patron Buddha. At first we were drawn to Avaloketeshvara as the Lord of Compassion, but we knew there was much more to this deity than what was written in most modern Tibetan spiritual books. One day I was walking in downtown Toronto and peered into an antique store that had some oriental statues and artifacts in the window. Venturing in, I saw an amazing statue of Avaloketeshvara, black in color, about four feet in height, with semi-precious gem stones and an aura of peace around it. To me it looked like museum quality. I knew the group had to have it. It was a lot of money, way more than what we could afford. We took up a collection from all the members and once we raised the money I went and bought it and brought it to our center. At first we put it into the main room, on the floor by a window. That night we had a meeting and by chance I was sitting in front of the statue with my back to it. As RN was teaching us, I was continually being bugged by an impression that the statue was unhappy. At first I thought this was weird, maybe it was just my imagination, but it continued until I had to interrupt RN and tell him what I was feeling.

We then moved the statue up to the second floor meditation room and offered incense. I no longer felt the statue being unhappy. We figured that this statue must have been in a temple at some time, maybe stolen from the temple during the Cultural

Revolution when many temples were destroyed in Tibet, and had some type of Deva force connected to it.

The photograph below is of this precious statue that was in the meditation room.

Statue in meditation room

So now we had two beautiful statues of Avalokiteshvara on our altar, one with an extra influence that seemed destined for us. We now had the mantra and the rupa, it was time to penetrate into the meaning. One thing we were inspired to understand is that the Path of Avalokiteshvara was in complete harmony with the teachings of the Master D.K. as given out by Alice Bailey.

In fact, the teachings of the Master D.K. are, if you will, an expression of the esoteric understanding of this unique form. Avalokiteshvara is the patron Buddha of the Trans-Himalayan Arhat School. Most people see this statue with its eleven heads and many arms as a beautiful work of cultural art. It's so much more! It is a Divine expression of a higher dimensional life manifested and expressed in our three-dimensional world. "In short, Avalokiteshvara literally interpreted means, 'the Lord that is seen'. It is, when correctly interpreted, in one sense, 'the *divine* Self perceived or seen by the *Self*,' the Atman or seventh principle ridded of its *mayavic* distinction from its Universal Source – which becomes the object of perception for, and by the *individuality* centered in *Buddhi*, the sixth principle, something that happens only in the highest state of *Samadhi*." (34) Each head represents a different loka, place or world of experience. The top three heads represent the world of Ishvara or gods. The second tier of heads represents the worlds of light or Heiranagarbha and the lower three heads correspond to our concretized physical universe or Visvanara. The arms holding the different implements such as the rosary and bow and arrow describe the different powers or how the compassion of Avalokiteshvara manifests. The hand holding the lotus can be seen as the power of evolution within our universe; everything is unfolding and evolving, all as one whole. To coincide with that, the hand holding the bow and arrow is the power to overcome all obstacles, fulfilling the planned evolutionary purpose. Another aspect of this statue is that it is standing and not sitting like most Buddhist statues. This must have some special purpose. This infers that Avalokiteshvara's power and purpose flows from the boundless light of Amitabha, the top head, down to the physical world of manifestation, the working out of some Divine scheme. In this sense, Avalokiteshvara acts as the Divine Mediator between the One Supreme and all of creation. An individual cannot contact the One Supreme, thus a mediator is needed to bridge the gap between the timeless and that which is in time. This is one of the deeper meanings of the Divine Christos. When you chant the mantra of Avalokiteshvara it is very helpful to also ponder on these meanings of this Divine expression. One thing that I must make very clear is that our insights into the meaning and power of Avalokiteshvara are not in line with the teaching that traditional Tibetan Lamaism has given out to the public. Our interpretation and insight is based on Theosophical esoteric principles and inspiration from the Masters.

Occult Insights

The awakened occultist becomes, in one sense, an expression of divine law, Vidya Maya. There are so many instances where religious followers or even aspirants claim that they have spoken to God. The occultist knows that this is illusion, or Avidya Maya. It's not possible once you have some understanding of the laws of super nature. Consider the following; God or that great Uni-being who created our solar system lives for an incomprehensible length of time but for the sake of discussion let's say he lives for 99 billion years. A human lives for 99 years. What is the proportion mathematically of this relationship of 99 billion years and 99 years? An entire human life seen from the reality awareness of God would not even register as a spark in time. It's like the Pacific Ocean being aware of what happens to a grain of sand. Another analogy to consider is using Niagara Falls to represent God and a Christmas light bulb represents man. Niagara Falls generates tremendous amounts of power. You cannot hook up a single light bulb to Niagara Falls unless the power is transferred and transformed through generators and many levels of transformers to an acceptable level of energy that the bulb is designed to receive in order to work. Our solar system works in a similar fashion. 'As above so below' is a very occult phrase and if pondered on, it helps us to see and make logical, determined concepts of the relationship between our physical world and the divine world. The Master D.K. even mentions that even the Buddha can only glimpse the purpose of THAT totality we incorrectly call God. Through history, Hindu yogis have experienced many different deities but they don't claim to talk to that totality that many religious followers of the Judeo-Christian faiths claim to speak to. When Lord Krishna, in his human form, blessed Arjuna with a vision of totality, Arjuna asked him to stop as it was too intense, too much. An enlightened

Buddhist may talk about 'sunyata' or the void as an absolute state, but they don't carry on conversations with it giving out sweet platitudes about being positive in life and to love yourself. Today there are still numerous mediums claiming to speak to higher, advanced beings of many varieties, yet if you take the time and study what they've said, there is very little knowledge, primarily platitudes about being good, the world is changing for the positive and we are all great potential, nothing you couldn't read in a book. Yet this is what people like to hear and want to hear. They want to know or believe God loves them. Though this God supposedly allows so much violence and death in our world through natural disasters, disease and war, they still want to believe God will care for them. The great Masters who were the force behind initiating the Theosophical Society gave out the esoteric doctrine to help educate humanity in order to break free of these false forms of spiritual thinking and superstitions, by translating the once hidden secrets of esoteric knowledge in a manner that could be understood by the Western intellect.

In Tibet

During Christmas of 1986, RN received, as one of his presents, a beautiful calendar for 1987 of Tibetan monasteries. Inside the calendar was an amazing picture of a statue of Avalokiteshvara, an incredible work of art, in the temple in Gyantse, Tibet. RN had a strong inspiration that I should go there, find this statue and meditate there. He thought the best time for me to go there would be during WESAK. So in May 1987 I went to Tibet via Hong Kong and Chengdu. Tibet had been closed to foreign tourists but was now open, so I could travel on my own; I just had to pay a little more as I didn't want to go on a guided tour.

Chengdu is a small Chinese city in Sichuan province, population of 8–10 million. Small for Chinese cities! Just outside of Chengdu, I went to an old Chinese Buddhist temple, the Temple of Divine Light. Having wandered through this very large and sprawling compound, I came across a Tibetan chapel. Turns out that many Tibetan lamas came through here in times past, as Chengdu was one of the old travel routes from Tibet to China. These temple altar rooms are not made for meditation. They are there so the public can offer incense, prayers and money. Since it was empty except for an old Chinese lady sitting on a stool at the back of the room, I stood in front of the altar and chanted. For some reason my voice seemed much higher, by an octave or so, than usual. I enjoyed this meditation of chanting as I felt uplifted and cleared somehow. I should mention that I had a driver and guide taking me around Chengdu for the day. The guide had come in to the chapel just as I was finishing my meditation. This old Chinese lady said to my guide, in Chinese, that my chanting sounded like an old Chinese instrument. I took that as a compliment.

The next day I flew to Lhasa, well close to it, as the airport is a two hour drive away from the capital. Compared to the old pictures of Lhasa, the Chinese have really built it up and modernized it. I stayed at a good hotel by 1987 Lhasa standards, which had oxygen tanks and masks in every room, since Lhasa is at 11,500 feet above sea level, plus a close circuit TV system. Once I was settled, I decided to go for a walk. The sun was just setting and the grey world of dusk was settling in. After walking for only 15 minutes, I felt a heaviness descend over me, making my head heavy with an uncomfortable pressure. Even my eyelids felt heavy. This was a different feeling than you get when you first try to walk around at a very high altitude shortly after arriving from sea level. I felt it was some type of an attack, what a welcome present. Eventually, I found a small temple behind the Potala palace. There was a small statue of Avalokiteshvara there and I stood in front of it and chanted for at least 30 minutes, until I felt the heaviness lift off of me. I could feel it being pushed off and the feeling of discomfort was immediately gone. Leaving the temple, I headed towards the downtown area and found a restaurant to eat in, after which I went back to the hotel. That night the "Sound of Music" was playing on the in-house close circuit TV, and the next night, too. The next day I took a tour of the Potala, which is now a museum. It is really something to see! There are many altar rooms with amazing statues of deities, lamas, saints and kings of Tibet. There is a definite mystical and peaceful feeling as you move from room to room. Many of the altar rooms are very dark, only lit by a few oil lamps that are kept burning around the clock. You get to see the room where the Dalai Lama lived before the Chinese took over. I would have liked to have meditated there but they keep you moving on the tour.

Then next day I took a local bus for the journey to Shigatse and from there I would head to Gyantse, where the statue was. I was the only non-local on the bus. At one point we went through a blinding blizzard as we bused over a mountain pass. The bus had only one windshield wiper that was barely working, so much so, that the bus driver kept sticking his hand out the side window and reaching around to wipe some snow of the front windshield. I don't think I was the only one who was scared on this trip, even the Tibetans on the bus seemed very anxious. The ride down from the pass was much scarier! Fortunately, as we descended a very steep grid, the snow storm seemed to abate. The bus was tearing down the side of this mountain, speeding along, hitting bumps, launching me and the other passengers out of our seats; I could hear metal-on-metal as the driver was applying the brakes. There was an audible 'sigh' of relief from everyone when we reached level ground and could safely continue, at a reasonable speed, on to Shigatse.

The monastery (Tibetan, gompa) at Shigatse was very large and still intact, having escaped the destructive violence of the Cultural Revolution. Not so in Gyantse, where only two of the main monastery buildings remained intact. I only stayed for two days, visiting the great monastery of Tashilumpo which was like a small town. There was a great statue of Lord Maitreya that many pilgrims were visiting on a daily basis while I was there. You would walk up these stairs to enter and circumambulate the statue and walk down another set of stair to exit. Next door there was a long altar room with many statues placed side by side. Here you would walk by these various statues of deities, offering incense and praying as you walked by. There was nowhere to sit or stop to meditate, as the flow of pilgrims seemed to be constant. I was a little frustrated by this as I thought there would be space to meditate in. Nothing really happened for me in Shigatse. It was a much smaller city than Lhasa and it had not seen too much of the modernization that Lhasa was experiencing. Other than Lhasa it was the only other city that had a hotel. The temple complex at Shigatse is one of the gems of the old Lama system. Even though it was as large as a small town, it was almost deserted. The monks I saw were those that cared for the various areas where the faithful would make offerings. I only stayed for two days and then got back on the bus to head to Gyantse which was around a four hour bus ride away. The bus ride to Gyantse was uneventful. The land we were driving through was very dry and dusty, almost like a desert, very barren. Snow-capped mountains could be seen in the distance but where we were driving was flat.

Gyantse was a very small town with two unpaved streets. It was so dusty! There wasn't even a proper hotel. At least Shigatse had a hotel. There were two sorts of guest houses. One was very small and everyone shared one big room. There were a few trekkers already there. I needed my privacy, so there was no way I was going to share. The next place was based on the same premise but was much larger and accommodated some of the tour buses that came through. Fortunately, it was presently empty. I had to buy up an entire room with all the beds to guarantee my privacy. It was just a room filled with cots, nothing more. The washroom was outside. Although it was May it wasn't that warm, especially in the mornings, and no hot water. It took me over a half-hour to walk to the monastery and I went twice daily. I found the statue of Avalokiteshvara (pictured above) in the main temple building of the Palchor Monastery. There were two chapels and one main hall, where the monks would chant, if there were any. In one of the chapels I found the statue that was pictured in the calendar that RN had shown me. I knew right away that this was where I was going to do my meditations. Again there was nowhere to meditate. In front of the statue of Avalokiteshvara was a large statue of Lord Maitreya in a seated posture. The devoted Tibetans would prostrate before the statue of Lord Maitreya and then circumambulate it, passing in front of the statue of Avalokiteshvara which was directly behind. If you stood in front of the statue of Lord Maitreya, you could not even see the statue of Avalokiteshvara, you had to move to the side to see it. The chapel was basically empty; there was only a young attendant monk there. I stood in front of the statue of

Avalokiteshvara and chanted.

Statue in temple at Gyantse

The temple was built in the 14th century, I believe, by one of
the disciples of Tsongkapa. I felt as if there was an opening to
a higher dimension in the chapel where I was chanting in front
of Avalokiteshvara. I had a strong feeling that at some time the
Master D.K. had been there, but that's just my feeling. I chanted
there twice every day for a week. My chanting seemed to soar,
lifting me upwards in thought and feeling. By the end of the

week of my chanting there, a small crowd of Tibetans were crowded around me watching as I chanted. One day, some Chinese soldiers came into the chapel and actually physically pushed me, indicating that I should stop chanting and leave. I held my ground firmly. The army retreated. I continued to come for a couple of more days and chanted in the same spot. I took a few pictures in this chapel and I was amazed when the film was developed that there was more there than I expected. It is interesting that Avalokiteshvara is the Divine Christos, the Mediator between the One Supreme and the Many in creation, and that in the above picture a cross of light should appear. Very few people have seen this picture, but I felt strongly that it should be included in the book. I should mention that, at this time, I was using a flash camera, a Nixon E, and that there was only a small oil lamp in front of the statue and one uncovered light bulb to illuminate the entire chapel. After about seven days, I returned by bus to Lhasa. I did a little touring, visiting a couple of the local monasteries, bought a Tibetan rug and a few gifts in the main market place before returning to Chengdu, then to Hong Kong and home. In Hong Kong I bought some more Buddhist statues, some for me and some for the group. When I returned home, RN said he could feel that my aura had been cleaned up a lot. I'm sure it was because of the week of chanting in Gyantse.

Advent of the Devas

One night, not long after RN was married, back in Indonesia, he awakened suddenly as his darkened room was filled with a radiant light. He saw and experienced an imposing figure ablaze with light moving towards him. He watched as if hypnotized as this figure seemed to put something into his wife's belly. When he awoke the next day, he didn't know what to make of this experience. His wife had no recollection of anything happening. RN felt and hoped that maybe a special, spiritual baby would now be born to him and his wife. A baby girl, Nadene, arrived almost nine months later, but as time went by she did not show any true spiritual inclinations, actually much the opposite. RN could not forget his experience and always questioned it and was puzzled by it, as he knew it was a true happening. He said it was too real and he knew it was not something that he imagined. Eventually, after a few years in Canada, Nadene, his daughter, had a baby boy. This child, Martin, was a typical little boy, more of a geek, not into sports but loved computers. He became very proficient with computers very quickly and with computer generated art. He loved to draw. I gave him some drawing lessons to help him with perspective and the correct proportions when drawing the human body. Around the time he was seven years old, he told RN that he was experiencing and seeing other beings that he realized no one else in our group could see. At first he was afraid to tell anyone. He was very shy. RN surmised that his grandson could see various Devas. Originally these Devas that he experienced were not that advanced and were very playful. The Devas would actually use Martin's body but Martin did not go into a trance. He was actually still attached to his body, but his consciousness would be just outside it, so to speak. Thus he was conscious of what was going on and could recall all that happened while the Devas were present. Trance mediums, on the other hand, black out when an entity uses their body and consequently do not recall what transpired in the interim. The danger of being a trance medium is that one surrenders their body and consciousness and therefore cannot distinguish what type of being is using them. Most trance mediums assume that it is some spiritually advanced being using them as a means to communicate with the physical world to give their message. As H.P.Blavatsky pointed out, they are generally a lower being, a ghost, an astral shell or lower Devic form, trapped between two worlds, looking for a means to contact earth life. That's why so much of the teachings that come from trance mediums are made up of basically sweet platitudes, no real direct instructions or deeper knowledge, and they never seem to know about the Masters of Wisdom.

RN could tell that they were genuine because the Devas could take negative elemental substances that he had absorbed out from his aura and 'clean' him. This helped him greatly at first, as sometimes it took hours of chanting to break down this negative, elemental lunar substance and the Devas could just do it instantly. Eventually, after a couple of years, greater, more advanced Devas started to use Martin's body and communicate with RN and even other group members. One great Deva was known as 'Zenma'. For some time, he was protecting Martin and the group. There were times when 'Zenma' was present; you could feel his powerful presence filling an entire room and talking through this child. Such Devas were warrior Devas, always battling negative forces of the left hand path and under the auspices of Avalokiteshvara and the Masters of Wisdom. RN had achieved such an advanced spiritual stage that the Devas were sent to cooperate with him in the work he was doing on the inner planes. Martin could see the Devas and describe them, but RN only could feel their presence and describe their main characteristics or qualities, based on his higher feelings. Not only did these Devas help RN with breaking down negative elemental substance, they also were able to teach him different mantras and how to use them. They helped with the battles and told RN that they actually absorbed more of the negative elemental substance than he did. Eventually, when Martin was 16 years old, some teachers and Masters started to use Martin's body in order to communicate with RN and the group. Some of these teachers were unknown to us, while others had places in history. Generally, if they helped you, you would notice a change immediately. Their instruction was precise and pointed at areas that you needed to work on. They did not give out positive platitudes to make your personality feel good about itself. For a while RN thought that Martin may turn out to be like H.P.Blavatsky.

As the daily attacks increased in intensity, RN appealed to the Devas for more 1st Ray mantra so he could continue to break down and dissolve the elemental residue that was left behind after an attack. When you are in a battle with elemental forces, the entire process of what happens is very esoteric and cannot be written about in exact detail. It's not allowed. The 1st Ray mantras that the Devas gave to RN were Hindu instead of Buddhist. Over time, RN started to turn from Buddhism to more Hindu studies. It almost seemed that he was returning to the direction that he had begun in before he started to chant to Avalokiteshvara. He was now learning Hindu mantras to help him in his battles. He said the Hindu mantras were more 1st Ray, more powerful than the Buddhist mantra, which made it easier to break down those substances that he was absorbing. Consequently, RN's knowledge and spiritual energy just increased at a very rapid rate. When RN chanted with you to help dislodge an elemental or lunar substance related to one's DOTH, you could instantly feel the power enter you and actually pull the elemental out or break down negative substance. When you got an elemental from one of the battles, you felt the astral substance swirling and you felt very blocked. So when RN pulled it out, all this chaotic feeling caused by the elemental stopped and you were back to your usual self. This is very esoteric work. Most aspirants on the Path haven't reached the stage yet where they can feel and discriminate between the various aspects of substance within their being that has to be transformed. When this occurred, RN would take the elemental, plus a small portion of your own negative past-life *kama-rupa* substance and burn it with the most suitable mantra. His aura became like fire. RN was now meditating and chanting eight or more hours a day. Most of us in the group meditated two hours a day. RN retired early because the spiritual demands on his life became too great. He found that even if he mixed with ordinary people, he was absorbing substances from them. That's why the Great Ones do not mix with humanity. The impurities would even be too great for them and hinder their work, therefore they stay on the higher planes or in the Himalayan vastness, out of the reach of the turmoil that is humanity.

When RN first started to dissolve elemental substance, it might have taken him a week to break down just one elemental. Years later, he could break down dozens of elementals in just one hour. The substance would filter through his physical body and the quintessence of the elemental life would be absorbed by his Essence. Thus, his Essence evolved and became stronger and stronger. This is how the aspirant becomes the adept and develops *siddhis* or occult powers. RN was no longer chanting to Avalokiteshvara but had incorporated other deities. Soon RN was chanting to Mother Kali and studying *The Gospel of Sri Ramakrishna* according to "M" as he was affectionately known. His real name was Mahendranath Gupta. This is a very large book, telling the day-to-day story of Sri Ramakrishna, his *sadhana*, his work with his disciples, and his relationship with the Divine Mother Kali. He said there was much more to gain from reading this book than the casual reader would see.

RN would cook pure vegetarian food for Mother Kali and then

offer it to her. After the offering was completed, we could then eat the offered food. It was amazing that we all felt much better after eating this special food, prasadam. You could distinctly feel the blessing from the Divine Mother Kali. Eventually, RN had to stop chanting to Mother Kali, as he said that her mantra was becoming too powerful for his body to sustain. Although I maintained my Buddhist discipline, I had many experiences of the Divine Mother Kali. This brought me back to my early experiences in Kolkatta, India, where I was continually seeing the image of the Divine Mother Kali but not understanding why and consequently tried to push them away. I now realized that I have some karmic affiliation with the Divine Mother. Many years later, when I was in India again, I went to a Kali temple during one of their sacred festivals to Mother Kali. Being pushed along in an overcrowded frenzy of pilgrims, just passing the altar, chanting one of the mantras to Mother Kali, I immediately felt her touch and blessing totally clean me out of a lot of negative kama-rupa substance. When I left the temple, I experienced a joyous feeling that was the grace of Mother Kali.

Dictates of Karma

For many years, since the beginning of the group, RN had wanted to build an esoteric school, a center for spiritual learning. He had planned a small center in the city, while the main esoteric school would be in the country on a large parcel of land with several houses and cottages. There would be an inner core group and several levels of aspirants, depending on their commitment and strength of their soul. One of the difficulties that we realized early on was that, as a group, we had gone too far into the esoteric world. The few new people that did come were instantly pulled into the 'cone of fire' of the existing group. Hardly any of these new aspirants could manage the impact of the group energy and were quickly flung out. This occurred for occult reasons, not personal reasons. They would be tested somehow very early on and if they were not able to overcome the hindrances evoked by the test, they would inevitably and usually quickly leave the group.

The group was protected by higher forces and only those who not only had karma with the group and its members, but also had karma with the school on the inner plane that we represented in the physical world, were able to come to the group. Thus, whenever we tried to find new members it was next to impossible. Very few people would come if we advertised an event like a lecture or meditation. This was a little disheartening for us for some time. When Martin grew older, he brought some of his friends to the group, but they seemed to be weak in their soul aspiration, even though they had karma with Martin. Then once the subjective world opened up and RN began to be attacked constantly in addition to taking on the negative karmas of his students, the possibility of having an esoteric school on a larger scale became dimmer and dimmer. Eventually, RN realized that having an esoteric school was his dream but the Masters had other plans for him: to battle these negative forces and in the process to become an adept. Thus, the group existed for the purpose of adding its quota of energy/shakti to RN's effort and because of the occult law of Divine-circulatory-flow between RN and the group, the members of the group were lifted up as if pulled by an invisible thread. Even members who were unable to maintain the degree of effort that the Group Work entailed and dropped out, would have made much more progress than if they had not been part of this experiment in Group Work.

By early 2000, the group had become very tight and close knit in an occult sense. Each individual knew what they had to do, both for themselves as aspiring souls and for the group. Each group member knew every other group member in an Essence intimacy, the beginning of true brotherhood, disciple relating to disciple. The Work became more esoteric and intense in discipline, to the point that we really couldn't discuss what we were doing with outsiders, even other spiritual people. We had passed through that invisible door that leads into the occult world of experiences which is not valued, believed in or even known by society in the world today. Thus, I have been instructed not to write about the more esoteric events that occurred later on up to the time of RN's passing in 2011.

Turn inward your mind,
And you will find your way. (35)

Our group was a blend of Theosophical knowledge and Vajrayana Tibetan Buddhism. The knowledge aspect was Theosophical, while our practice was Vajrayana with focus on *Mantrayana*. Initially we focused most of our time on studying, to get a deeper understanding of the Work, building a strong framework, in the end, we stressed more the practice, going from the 'eye doctrine' to the 'heart doctrine', as taught in the short esoteric fragment, *The Two Paths* by H.P.Blavatsky. As the group spiritually evolved, many things became clear to us that were mere words before. You really start to see the flow of life on this planet from a different point of view. An interesting example has to do with what the Master D.K. discusses about the inner drive, through the entire cosmos, towards some goal. On our planet this is the force that drives everything forward, the force of evolution that permeates all life. Man is asleep and doesn't see these forces and how they are always there. I'm not just talking about Darwin's theory of evolution. This is the evolution of 'consciousness', leading to the awakening and knowledge of the Soul. Most creatures on this planet walk forwards, not backwards. Man, for instance, walks on the land not on water. Day and night follow in sequence and so life also follows this sequence. To explain the above statements, life moves forward and is expanding, thus this archetype manifests in almost all creatures; therefore we walk forward, symbolizing our alignment with this plan of evolution that is always moving forward. To walk requires the overcoming of friction between the ground and us trying to move forward. Thus, evolution moves forward through the overcoming of diverse hindrances in nature. Overcoming friction is necessary to make progress. It is the same with meditation. The human body acts as a resistance, pain, discomfort and blockages are necessary for spiritual evolution. This is one of the reasons the Buddhist teaching declares that if you have a human body do not waste your life away on 'samsaric sensations' but instead it is better to enter the Dharma. Devas do not evolve in the same way as man. They evolve through an unconscious alignment to Divine Law following its directives, thus their evolution is much slower than human evolution but they live for aeons. Humanity, on the other hand, evolves through the overcoming of friction, using resistance to find an inner harmony and to awaken to the purpose of Divine Law and to learn its mysteries. Thus life is made to move forward. Look at so many organizations in the world which run on the same principle. Once you're a member in an organization, industrial, educational, athletic, you try to grow, getting promotions, a higher belt, a better rank and greater success. All this is the inherent force of natural evolution – moving all forward over vast periods of time, so that some unseen plan reaches a fulfillment that affects our totality of life.

The Esoteric Work is not as people assume. Esoteric literature, such as the works of the Tibetan Master D.K., tend to paint a very glowing picture of the Path. Other books on Yoga or Mysticism talk in such an illumined manner of enlightenment, the Path of Non-doing or becoming One with the All. This in itself is an illusion and yet is necessary. Aspirants to whatever path think they can achieve enlightenment or non-doing, as a group of Taoist aspirants claimed in their teaching. The truth is that the idea of enlightenment is like the bait on a hook that is thrown into the waters of life to catch potential aspirants. Enlightenment is far, far away! Very few books actually give a true indication of the intensity of the struggle and focused unending discipline, plus the heartache and pain that a disciple must undergo on the Path of Transformation. There are a few books such as the story of *Milarepa, Tibet's Greatest Yogi, Ramakrishna and his Disciples, Blossom and the Fruit* and *Empty Cloud the story of Xu Yun*. All illustrate the struggles that these advanced disciples underwent in order to realize the great mystery of life. One of the problems today is that because of our technological advancement and higher levels of education, we've developed an arrogance, thinking that today there must be shortcuts to the Path of Awakening. Our techno-materialistic-oriented-educated lifestyle has created a lopsided psychological development in us. The spiritual path beckons us to awaken and develop our Being-ness to help counterbalance this present social trend. The Ageless Wisdom is unchanged. It requires work, that's why it is called the '*Great Work*'. Maybe that's why Helena P.Blavatsky wrote in the introduction of the *Voice of the Silence: "dedicated to the few"*.

The Great Work to be done is summarized in a simple phrase known as the 'Watch words of the Disciple'.

TO KNOW * TO WILL * TO DARE * TO BE SILENT

The Group Work: Part 2 Practice

The Dharma of words from sutras, texts and all the articles and writings on this vast subject exist for the *Dharma of Practice*. Practice is the root for attaining not only a truer understanding of the spiritual work, but also is the means to apply what you've read and learned. Through the discipline of practice, in time, you become a 'knower', and can verify that what you've read about is actually true. Without practice the Dharma is just theory. The mind can only get a glimpse of the truth. With practice the Dharma becomes an expanding reality. Practice takes you into the world of psychic feeling and knowing, whereas relying just on reading various works of the Dharma only builds one's pride and a spiritual personality, which in fact becomes adharma, or not dharma. The understanding of the Science of Yoga can be applied to any religious type of mysticism or occult spiritual development. The Science of Yoga, the *Yoga Sutras* of Patanjali are a study of the psychology of the mind that goes light years beyond what contemporary psychologists know of the mind today.

Below I've outlined some of the techniques that we used successfully in the group. These techniques are a stepping stone to deeper understanding and experience. These means of practice *do work* but that doesn't mean instantly. The Work is not microwaveable! Practice and the discipline of practice (sadhana) take years of constant effort and fine tuning. We are all different but these techniques were developed to suit everyone who is willing to undergo the necessary discipline. If you don't see results after two months, then continue for a year, if after a year you are still in the dark then continue for another year. If you can do that, then you are making progress, it just may not be how you imagined it should be.

Technique #1: Pratyahara – How to withdraw from the senses.

In the Astanga Yoga, as outlined by Patanjali in the Yoga Sutras, *pratyahara* is the first of the 'inner' yoga disciplines. It means the ability to withdraw one's awareness away from the senses or the outer world, inwards to a point of conscious awareness. In one sense the outer world fades away from one's awareness as one is totally focused inwards. There are many levels in *pratyahara*, from the beginner to the one who can enter this stage of experience instantly. Achieving *pratyahara* is not something that is done just one or two times. For a long time it is a constant discipline, it has to be mastered, but eventually *pratyahara* becomes a regular state and one can tune into it as soon as one focuses the attention. When it becomes a regular state of being, then one has achieved a definite *'center of gravity'*. It is a gradual development and a skill, just as leaning to fly an airplane or walk a tightrope are also skills that take time and effort to learn, only *pratyahara* requires more patience and perseverance. The main point to understand with *pratyahara* is that you are learning to redirect the flow of force within your mind, to counter the natural tendency or habitual patterns of forces in the mind from an outwards to an inwards movement. Force has to be re-directed not stopped. Trying to stop the flow of mental movements is like trying to stop rushing water after the dam has broken. You can re-direct it but it's very hard to stop.

In the diagrams below, diagram A shows the flow of force, life force, from a central point outward. This force flows outward primarily because our senses are in constant contact with our environment.

Force constantly flows out through the senses so the personality can be in contact with the outer world. The personality exists on the rim of the wheel. The inner circle represents the inner self which acts as a distributor of soul force that flows out to

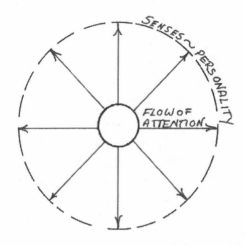

(Diagram A) From the Self to the 'not-self'.

the periphery, the personality. This is what nature has intended. The yogi has to overcome this and through yoga technology will increase or accelerate spiritual development.

In the second stage (diagram B) this same force is being redirected back to the center or self, Essence. This is achieved through visualization and focusing, thus creating a central point of tension or a center of awareness. It's a fascinating challenge, but through steady effort one will see definite results. Sometimes, though, you'll feel too tired to make the effort or external circumstances will make it more difficult to concentrate. There is always a challenge to overcome obstacles. Watch the results of your daily effort and how this exertion affects you emotionally and mentally. Make notes. In time you will see that through this Work you begin to awaken an inner spiritual will. That's why the Master D.K. calls this effort 'kurushetra' or the battleground. It is the effort and discipline that you make every day overcoming all hindrances that **IS** the experience. Your ever-flowing mind becomes your teacher.

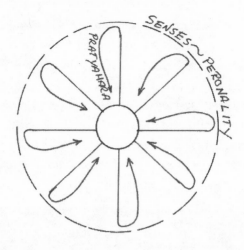

(Diagram B) Centering: Creating a 'center of gravity'.

Visualize a golden flame or radiant sun, or even just a point (this could prove to be too intense) in the area of the heart chakra, try to hold the visualization steady, and detach from the ever-flowing thoughts. Do not get caught by your thoughts. If you find yourself lost in some group of thoughts that trapped your attention, STOP and start again. As you get stronger with this simple exercise, you'll get a working concept of what *pratyahara* is. By this method you withdraw your attention inwards, back to the center, the inner self, your true Essence. This is the first stage.

(Diagram C) Double pointed arrow, See the Seer.

In this stage of *pratyahara* (diagram C) the arrow becomes a double pointed arrow. This arrow going from the 'seer' (the one who is seeing), follows with the act of seeing the object and then from the object the arrow at the same time is coming back to the seer, meaning that the seer is aware or seeing himself. This is seeing in *both* directions at the same time. This is the first stage of real *Self-Remembering*. The next step is to *'feel the feeler'*, a deeper stage of Self-Remembering. When you can do this you're making very good progress with your meditation.

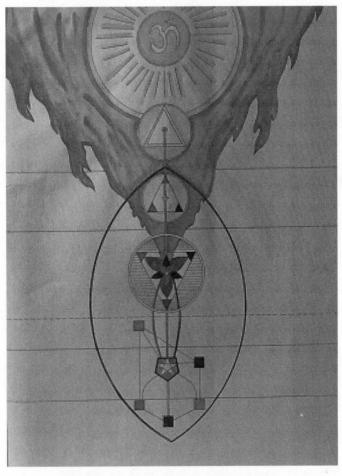

Atma Vidya diagram, painting by author.

Technique #2: Mediation – Atma Vidya or the *Occult Constitution of Man.*

Spirit, Soul and Personality.

This drawing or mandala of Atma Vidya has many uses for those wanting to develop a better working understanding of Esoteric Psychology. It can be used as both a meditation and as a study tool. Before using Atma Vidya as a meditation tool it is best to have at least a basic understanding of the philosophy and workings of this esoteric map.

1) From the OM the radiant expression of the One Life and Light on the first plane 'Adi', though there are many rays, we'll follow ONE ray as it moves (down) through the planes of manifestation.

2) On the 2nd plane of 'Anupadaka' this ONE ray differentiates from the One Life and Light and the Monad (Father) appears. This is the first differentiation or separation.

3) The ONE ray continues and Atma, Buddhi, Manas, the higher triad, come to be on their respected planes; at its core is the 'Hiradaya' or 'Heart'. Then this ONE ray continues further and deeper into matter. This ONE ray comes to rest as the Jewel in the Lotus.

4) The Causal or Soul body with the three permanent atoms and the three-fold lotus and a hidden inner lotus surrounding the 'Jewel in the Lotus' on the 3rd sub-plane of the Mental plane. Then the desire for form life awakens and this individualized Soul life sends down its ray of life and light.

5) Then the lower triangle, made up of the mental unit or intellectual center on the lower mental plane, including the emotional unit on the astral plane, down to the physical/etheric body on the physical plane.

6) Finally, at the center of the lower triangle, the hexagram/symbol of the personality that surrounds the 5-pointed

star, symbol of the Essential Nature, with radiant lines of force and prana reaching to the three aspects of the lower triangle. The 5-pointed star is always upright; the upper point signifies consciousness controlling the other lower points which symbolize the elements.

7) Note the Ida and Pingala from the Causal Body that connect to the 5-pointed star and the Sushuma connecting the Higher Self to the lower self.

In the meditation you begin the visualization by picturing the flame in the heart. Watch the Flame, the Now and the breath. Remember, thoughts cannot move in the Now. Now visualize the vault of space, emptiness. Hold the visualization of space, the Now and the breath. In this space, visualize a tiny point of tremendous energy. Then this point explodes into radiant light, energy and electricity. The point grows and becomes a ball of fire, a golden white ball of fire radiating tremendous energy and light. The ball of fire expands into a blazing sun. All thoughts are burned in the flames of the sun, the radiant golden sun with many rays of light. Feel the tremendous energy of the sun radiating love and light. Now from the blazing sun radiates one ray.

1) From the sun sound the OM audibly 3 times and then silently 3 times.

2) Picture one ray descending to the Monad, visualize this as a tiny, golden-white triangle.

3) Then visualize Atma, Buddhi, and Manas with the Hiradaya as a small radiant sun in the center. Again sound the OM as before.

4) Now visualize the causal body, then the lotus within the triangle of the permanent atoms, the 1st outer lotus, the knowledge petals, and then the love petals and sacrifice petals. Ponder on the meaning of the lotus petals. Picture

a radiant golden white jewel emerging from the last petals that hide it. Again sound the OM as in step #1.

5) Next visualize the mental unit and contemplate its characteristics, the same with the emotional body on the astral plane, finishing with the physical etheric body.

6) Finally visualize the Essential Nature as the radiant golden 5 pointed star. As you hold this visualization, realize that you are not your physical body, emotions, and thoughts. Then focus on and hold this seed thought, "I'm an Eternal Soul, a Sacred flame within the greater Divine flame". Sound the OM as in #1.

7) Now reverse the sequence and climb back up to the radiant sun and finish by sounding the OM as in #1. When you reach the 1st plane of Adi, visualize that you are engulfed in the radiant golden light of the OM. All that now exists is your *feeling* of individualized conscious awareness within the One Life and Light.

Technique #3: **The Five Buddhas' of Transformation, Dhyani Buddhas.**

The meditations and disciplines of the Five Buddhas of Transformation require a focused mental effort with feeling to penetrate into their meaning, not just memorizing their names or powers. Memorizing their names and meanings is necessary at first to help organize this teaching in your mind. In time, a concept or thought-form of the teaching can be built up, which then can be applied, reaching up to the reality of the Five Buddhas of Transformation.

There are several traditional methods of meditation using these archetypical Buddhas. There is a circular pattern as indicated by the arrows in the diagram below. Start with Aksobhya then move to Ratnasambhava, then to Amitabha, then Amogasiddhi and finishing with Vairocana. Another method of entering the mandala, start with Aksobhya then move to Amitabha, then Ratnasambhava, to Amogashiddi and then finish with Vairocana.

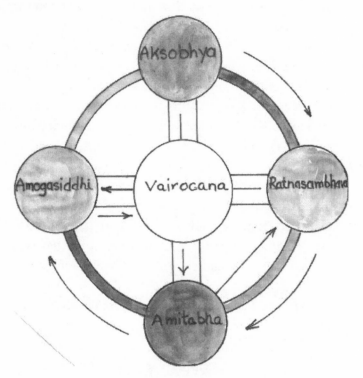

Diagram of <u>Five Dhyani Buddhas,</u>
painting by author.

1) Let's start by creating a visual mandala of the Five Buddhas of Transformation around us. Begin by visualizing Aksobhya Buddha in front, deep blue in color, his right hand is reaching down touching the ground (bhumisparsa mudra), his left hand is lying open on his lap, holding a lotus. Touching the earth in this case means solidarity, unshakeable, solid like a mountain. Nothing in heaven or earth can shake the resolve and meditation of Aksobhya. The Wisdom of Aksobhya is, 'Mirror like, reflecting ev-

erything in the universe'. A mirror only reflects, it is not touched or moved by what it reflects. Events happen, but Aksobhya is unmoved, and remains detached. His mind is clear, pure awareness. His power is the 'all Seeing Eye', which means his awareness is bright and penetrates everywhere. Picture Aksobhya above your head and then draw it down over you and become Aksobhya. Feel your total being become like Aksobhya, unshakeable, solid like a mountain, able to withstand whatever life throws at you. Take on the characteristics of Aksobhya, let go of your personality. As Aksobhya you can sound the OM silently to help maintain the visualization.

2) The next Buddha, Ratnasambhava, is visualized on your right side. His color is radiant gold. Ratnasambhava sits with his right hand open, palm up reaching out in front (dana mudra), while the other palm lies open on his lap holding a beautiful diamond. The Wisdom of Ratnasambhava is 'perfect equanimity and balance'. His power is the 'all embracing Mother', that brings perfect peace. Ratnasambhava has the unique power of being able to reach out and transform any agitation or disharmony into peace and equanimity. As in step #1 become Ratnasambhava. All disquiet and tensions are transformed by the transformative harmonizing power of Ratnasambhava. Radiate the OM, feeling a liquid golden light of warmth and peace fill your entire nature.

3) Now let's visualize behind us the Buddha Amitabha. His color is flaming red-orange like the setting sun. His hands are folded in the familiar meditation (dhyana) mudra on his lap. On most of the pictures of the Buddha we see, where he is sitting peacefully in meditation, his hands folded on his lap, showing the Buddha Gautama reflect-

ing the quality of Amitabha. The Buddha Gautama, the historical Buddha, is in fact the human (Manusha) form of Amitabha, over-shadowed by this Divine archetype that exists eternally in 'Alaya' the Universal Store Consciousness. The Wisdom of Amitabha cuts through all illusion of existence in form, as his awareness penetrates through flowing time, cutting even a 'ksana' the smallest moment in time. His power, 'Pandara' makes things transparent in order to see through the Mayas and illusions of embodied existence to the inner truth of all things. As in step #1 become Amitabha. Now contemplate what it means to cut through flowing time. If you could, what would be the result? Think deeply!

4) On your left side, visualize Amogashiddhi, emerald green in color. His right hand is raised in the mudra of power, (abhaysa) mudra holding the double Dorje, or Visa-vajra. This mudra of fearlessness and power shows that he has power over all natural forces in manifestation. Consequently, Amogasiddhi is the most powerful of the Five Buddhas of Transformation on the physical plane. The Wisdom of Amogashiddi is 'all accomplishing wisdom that manifests as perfect magical action at the right moment'. His power or shakti is the green Tara, who has the power to make things happen and even alter one's karma. Maitreya, the Buddha of the Future, will be the Manusha Buddha of Amogasiddhi. As in step #1, become Amogashiddhi. When you can feel and connect with the wisdom of Amogashiddhi then, when life throws you some difficult choices, use the power and wisdom of Amogasiddhi to guide you.

5) The last and central Buddha in this mandala is Vairocana. Visualize Vairocana above you in the center of the man-

dala. Vairocana means blazing white like the sun at noon, therefore his color is radiant white. His hands are in the 'Dharmachakra' mudra the symbol of 'turning the wheel of the law or teaching'. The motion from Sunyata, the void, the unmanifest to Samsara, the world of time and space is the wisdom of Vairocana. His power is 'all embracing space', where the blazing white light of Vairocana penetrates all existence from the tiniest atom to the entire galaxy. As in step #1, become Vairocana, except make the visualization a brilliant, radiant, golden white, dissolving all thoughts, worries, fears, and hope. All is dissolved in the radiance of Vairocana.

The mystery and knowledge of the Five Buddhas of Transformation is very deep and can be applied in many ways. The five skandas of clinging are transformed through these five great Buddhas, as are the five poisons. Which Buddha is associated with which skanda, which poison? You have to figure this one out yourself through meditation. You can also penetrate deeper into the knowledge of the 'five Bardos,' or in-between states when you understand which Bardo is represented by which of the Five Buddhas of Transformation. The door to many mysteries can be unlocked by meditating deeply on these Five Buddhas. Through the discipline of meditating on the Five Dhyani Buddhas, your power of visualization, concentration and centering will increase dramatically. Also, with this meditation, the opportunity exists to connect with a higher power, to touch some aspect of their reality, which brings knowledge and wisdom. I remember one student who had been meditating on these Five Buddhas telling me that once, all of a sudden, the Buddhas became larger than life, surrounding her with a feeling of protection and awe. She felt inspired to make greater effort, to be able to reach again that indescribable feeling of inner joy.

Now, let's look at some practical applications for day-today transformation. Before we begin, I want to point out that these applications do not come easily. This meditation requires a strong discipline and a certain degree of alignment has to be achieved. Once you've studied these Five Buddhas, try to feel which Buddha you feel closest to. Then, spend more time focusing on that Buddha and its attributes. The purpose of visualizing yourself as one of the Dhyani Buddhas is to draw down a higher power to help to control the lower mind. You cannot stop your thoughts but they can be redirected and set to a new rhythm.

Situation (1) It's been a stressful day at work; it seems that everybody wants something from you at the same time. You are beginning to feel unglued, anger is growing and you feel that any moment now you'll blow your top like some old volcano. It is at this precise moment, as the pressure is building, that you immediately visualize yourself as the Buddha Aksobhya. For the time it takes to inhale deeply and exhale slowly, feel yourself as Aksobhya. As you visualize, feel the qualities of Aksobhya become unshakeable, solid, unmoved by outside events, like a great cosmic mirror. With practice this can eventually happen quickly. By making this connection and feeling yourself as Aksobhya, you automatically detach from the harmful identification with the negative emotion of anger. With practice, the feeling of peace and stability that Aksobhya gives will increase and the strength of your tendency for irritability and anger will, in time, diminish. Try to hold the feeling of Aksobhya for at least three to five minutes, if it is possible. You can practice this whether in an office, the subway, or even at a party. Nobody has to know what the 'inner you' is up to. Just try to slip away for those few minutes to increase your feeling as Aksobhya.

Situation (2) In another situation, you are working on a difficult problem and you feel blocked, unable to get any type of results or answers. It can be any type of problem, whether studying for an exam, something at work, or a personal creative project. Then visualize yourself as the Buddha Amitabha. Concentrate on Amitabha's power of making things transparent to see the truth and cut through all illusions. Have Amitabha help you solve a problem, helping to awaken the higher mind to see outside the box. Amitabha helps to clear away the metal fog that seems to hinder the mind's creativity. This effort opens you to inspiration or an AHA! moment.

Technique #4 **Chanting a Mantra.**

What is the deeper meaning of the mantra, OM MANI PADME HUM? Usually this mantra is translated as, "OM, hail, the jewel in the lotus, HUM". What does this tell us? Nothing! To understand this mantra involves a great deal of knowledge about the occult constitution of man and his relationship to deity. To start, I will discuss each word of the mantra. 1) **OM:** The 'OM' is called in Sanskrit, 'Pranava'. For a mantra it indicates that the origins of the mantra are from the ONE source, the One Life and Light, Ishvara, Logos or God. It further means that it comes from this One Source down to earth. There are mantras that do not start with the 'OM'. One should be cautious of a mantra that does not start with the 'OM'. 2) **MANI:** Translates as 'jewel'. What jewel is this mantra focused on? The jewel in this mantra is the 'spark' of spirit or life that is embedded and hidden within the subtle energy (Shakti) of Deva substance within the Causal body/Soul (karana sharira, vijnana maya kosha). This causal body or Soul exists in the subtle matter of the 'tajas tatwa' or the 3rd/2nd sub-plane of the mental plane. Though we cannot see it, it exists and has form, it is sometimes called, '*the formless form*'. The Causal Body or Soul is the vehicle of Spirit, just as the physical body is the vehicle for the Soul. This 'jewel' hidden within the heart of the Causal Body is the focal point of the One Life or Monad which lies dormant and has to be awakened by the aspirant through the process of Initiation. 3) **PADME**: This Lotus is the energy or Shakti aspect within the Causal body (see diagram of Atma Vidya) that grows as each physical incarnation is experienced. This lotus encloses the 'jewel', thus it's called the 'Jewel in the Lotus'. The lotus evolves from a closed bud surrounding the Jewel to an open radiant flower, revealing the Jewel at the point of liberation when the advanced aspirant, now a yogi, is about to become an 'Arhat', an Enlightened One. 4) **HUM**: The 'hum' is a complex word within this mantra formula. It means to integrate. When chanting OM MANI PADME HUM, on the HUM you feel your little 'I' integrating with the greater Divine stream that carries you upwards/ inwards to the higher planes (lokas) of the deity. Of course, the term 'upwards' is relative in time and space in this application. OM MANI PADME HUM is a very sacred mantra. It's the fire of the One Life and Light that comes down to awaken and evolve the Lotus of the Soul, leading to the liberation of the Divine Spark, re-integrating it back into that expression of Divinity we call Avalokiteshvara or Chenrizig.

To chant this mantra properly one has to feel themselves as the individualized unit of consciousness, the Essential Nature, separate from the personality but yet initially guided by the will aspect of one's 'manasa vijnana' or higher mind, connected with the breath and the visualization of the deity. Avalokiteshvara acts as a bridge between the One Supreme and the many in incarnation. The meaning and purpose of Avalokiteshvara and OM MANI PADME HUM is so much more than what the Tibetan Lamas will tell you. Understanding its deeper meaning actually helps you to achieve deeper results.

When you want to chant
1) First, feel as *centered* in your Essential Nature as you can.
2) Next, focus on the flame or visualize Avalokiteshvara

clearly.
3) Inhale and chant with the exhale. Maintain the visualization and feeling.

Do not rush! Best to do it slowly, re-focusing each time. Remember, it is the higher feeling of devotion, surrender and renunciation that has to be generated as you chant. You don't want to be just a tongue waging. Don't push the mantra. If you notice your body tensing up, stop...relax and start again.

If you chant a mantra like OM Mani Padme Hum regularly, you are creating a relationship between the deity and yourself. Over time, as your astral body is purified, the shakti (energy) of the deity begins to permeate through your being. In general there are different rules for each deity. Some are easier to communicate with while others much more difficult. Some require the aspirant to maintain a different diet, use particular incense, or offerings. Offerings are very important, but that's an entirely different matter. Once you become aligned to a mantra then the note of that mantra becomes more ingrained into your being. You will become more sensitive to your environment, especially music. If you listen to the wrong music, for instance, it can counter the good that you've built up and you can even lose your connection temporarily with the deity. Your connection with the deity becomes *sacred*, a mystical marriage, all important as you make progress on the Path.

So a mantra and deity are 'one'. If you build up a relationship with a Buddhist deity, you cannot just on a whim switch to chanting a Hindu mantra. This can create problems.

There are four levels of mantra:
1) Mechanical repetition (vaikhari),
2) Entering into the stream or energy of the mantra (madhyama), mantra/shakti.
3) Obtaining the power of the mantra (pashanti)

4) Not for us humans but when the deity chants (para).

We all start with mechanical repetition. To make progress, we have to reach the second level. Each level has secondary levels. Mantrayana is the core of Vajrayana. Mantrayana leads to the Path of Initiation. Mantrayana invokes the Deities, the Solar Pitris. It is the most secret knowledge that is passed on from an initiate to the disciple, the Sacred Whispered teaching.

Brahman = Absolute = Sunyata = Tao

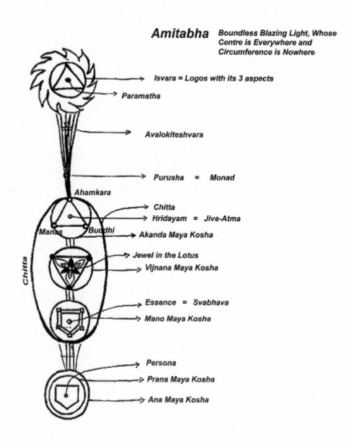

Amitabha *Boundless Blazing Light, Whose Centre is Everywhere and Circumference is Nowhere*

Isvara = Logos with its 3 aspects

Paramatha

Avalokiteshvara

Purusha   =   Monad

Ahamkara

Chitta
Hridayam   =   Jiva-Atma
Manas   *Buddhi*   *Akanda Maya Kosha*

Jewel in the Lotus
Vijnana Maya Kosha

Chitta

Essence   =   Svabhava
Mano Maya Kosha

Persona
Prana Maya Kosha
Ana Maya Kosha

Man's Divine Mystery

The above chart by RN is based more on Yoga Vidya of the

Sankya Yoga system, showing the various 'kayas' or sheaths, such as the 'Ana Maya Kosha' which translates as the illusory body created by food.

The chart below is an amalgamation of Theosophical, '4th Way' and Yoga teachings. By being inclusive, in this respect, more knowledge is covered and there are fewer missing links, so to

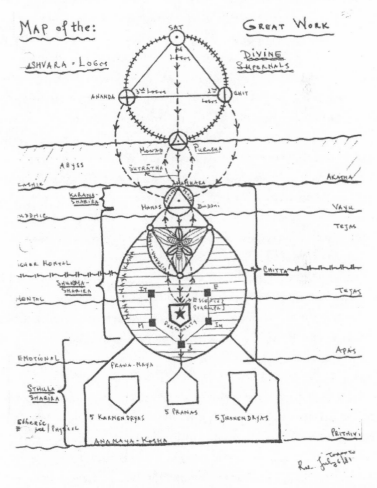

The Great Work

Chart drawn by RN

speak, in the knowledge that each discipline gives out.

This is the chart of the "*Great Work*" that illustrates a total conceptual presentation of the philosophy of esoteric science. It shows that from the ONE LIFE, which is shown by the OM, manifest the Seven Rays of Creation. These Seven Rays radiate to the Monad reflected in the Hiradya, shown here as the heart of the Triad of Atma, Buddhi, Manas. From the monad, the sushumna unites the triad with the causal body or soul, which includes the lotus petals and permanent atoms, then down to the pentagram representing the Personality and finally to the five-pointed star that represents the reflection of the soul, the soul in incarnation which I call the Essential Nature. The expression of the personality is shown via the five centers. All is contained within the Chitta or 'mind-stuff'. In the esoteric world, all is within the mind. Also included within the physical body are the five karmendryas (hands, feet, speech, organs of reproduction and excretion), five pranas and five jnanendryas (senses). The five planes of evolution are divided into higher and lower. This chart is excellent, as it gives you a total map. Remember, this is only a two dimensional representation of a 4th dimensional idea.

In the chart opposite, RN is blending Zen concepts with a little known Buddhist knowledge of the eight Vijnanas. The eight Vijnanas are mentioned in the Lankavatara and Avatamsaka sutras of the Buddha. There is very little information on these eight Vijnanas. Vijnana is defined as consciousness, thus the eight Vijnanas are the eight levels of consciousness in the Buddhist system. On the right side of the chart are the five stages of Zen awakening lined up to the diagram of the eight Vijnanas. The first five Vijnanas relates to the five senses. Each sense has its consciousness. The sixth Vijnana is the consciousness level of the personality, while the seventh Vijnana is at the level of the soul. The eighth Vijnana is called 'Alaya' which is translated as 'store consciousnesses'. This part is quite straight forward but to

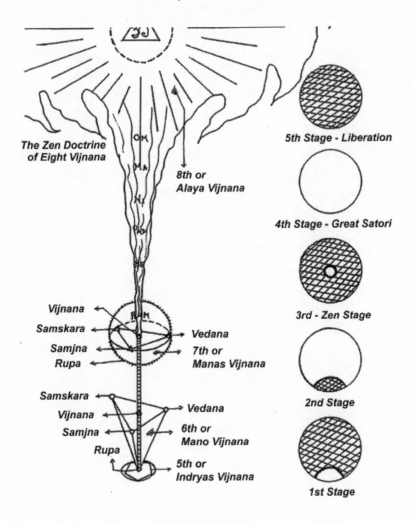

Five stages of Zen

Chart drawn by RN

understand the esoteric significance of this system you have to blend the eight Vijnanas with the five Skandas, which is done in the chart. Then an entire new world of ideas awakens.

For instance, in Buddhism there is no teaching on the soul or 'vijnana maya kosha' as there is in the Hindu systems and the broader Theosophical teachings. But if you want to understand on a deeper level contemplate how 'rupa skanda', the form aspect exists on the seventh Vijnana. Thinking along this line you can see right away that 'rupa' on the seventh Vijnana must be the soul or causal body of the teachings of both Yoga and the Master D.K. This means that in the esoteric aspect of Buddhism there is a 'soul'.

Therefore, for meditation, the seeker should be able to center their feeling of 'I' in the Seventh Vijnana which then puts you in your Essence, aligned to both your Soul and Hierarchy.

The Seven Rays

The Seven Rays are a profound esoteric teaching on the seven radiant qualities of that Greater Life that is our Solar system. Relative to our planet, earth, they originate within the Solar Logos. Yet we are told, in the works of Alice Bailey, that they actually originate from outside of our Solar System and work through the Solar Logos. These great powers, seven types of force, imbued with consciousness and life, color and condition, characterize and help to guide the cosmic forces of evolution from the Solar system, inclusive of all existing life, including man, on this planet. The Seven Rays are cyclic in manifestation and generally there are only Five Rays that are active at any one time on earth.

The Seven Rays also present a unique method of psychological insight. Each aspect of a human being is an expression of one of the Seven Rays. Our bodies, personalities, even our Souls. If you have a Second Ray soul, Sixth Ray personality and a First Ray body, this information paints a clear picture of this individual. They are expressions of energies of each Ray, with its own coloring or characteristics. One must be able to *feel* the quality of each of the Rays in order to gain the insights needed to make this system of psychology practical. In Part 1 of this book I use the Seven Rays in a descriptive manner to give the reader some insight into their usage. Below is a simple outline including the name and characteristics of each of the Seven Rays.

First Ray: **Will and power**: See the First Ray like a welder's torch, a focused flame that cuts through everything. The First Ray is used to break down forms to make way for new forms to evolve. A truly First Ray personality is very rare. Usually a Sixth Ray personality with a First Ray sub-ray will manifest as a general during wartime or as a destructive tyrant.

Second Ray: *Love Wisdom*: This Second Ray is radiant, expansive and warming, and yet it is the power that holds or binds together. The Second Ray quality of the love of family holds the family together. An aspect of Divine Love is gravity that holds all in place. An expression of compassion and a charity to all is a Second Ray quality.

Third Ray: *Creative Intelligence*: The Creative Intelligence of the Third Ray is seen in higher mathematics that touch on the great laws of our planetary system. Abstract thought that peers into the flow of the great laws that govern all life is a quality of the Third Ray. The circulatory flow of the Third Ray can also be seen in activity of the worlds' finances and business.

Fourth Ray: *Harmony Through Conflict*: The splash of colors in a painting on some material like a dress or in fashion is an expression of the Fourth Ray. Art is a visual balance between light and shade and form. When this balance is achieved there is harmony and beauty. A beautiful sunset, a panoramic mountain view or a display of fireworks all express the Fourth Ray. Romantic songs as they express the sadness, joys and yearning for love are the Fourth Ray that is so active today.

Fifth Ray: *Concrete Knowledge*: Applying the laws of energy into viable forms that function, like the works of an engineer who plans and implements the law of hydraulics to create the power to cause the massive shovels on giant excavators to dig up tons of earth. The Fifth Ray is the quality of exact science; you need it in manufacturing technology and in the deeper occult sciences.

Sixth Ray: *Idealism and Devotion*: Holding to the form, focused intent, unchanging direction, soldiers on the march and perseverance through all types of hardship, all express the Sixth Ray. Sincere devotion, whether to a political ideal or a religious belief, is an expression of the Sixth Ray.

Seventh Ray: *Ceremonial Order:* Everything has its place. At work everyone has their place, whether it's in the office or on the assembly line. This daily routine which is performed in every organization is an expression of 'ceremonial order'. Large organizations, corporations, military and even religious orders come under the Seventh Ray. Today the Seventh Ray is very powerful, conditioning the routines of our daily lives from business to religion.

Part 3 Appendix

Picture of RN taken by author (2005)

Lecture by R.N. – November 28, 1981

The Science of Transformation in the Great Work

Many aspirants on the Path of Light wonder at a certain point in their development – after years of studying different kinds of Teaching, collecting knowledge of Yoga, Buddhism, the Kabbalah, Vedanta etc., either from books or from listening to so-called teachers – why, even though they have gathered quite a lot of information about the Teaching, they remain dissatisfied and feel that they have not found what they are searching for... they have not encountered the Great Wonder.

Indeed, knowledge or information obtained only from books or mediocre teachers is not enough as it *cannot bring about a transformation in our being.* All the data we have gathered has to be understood with the Essence/Soul and "distilled" into real Esoteric Knowledge, which is beyond words and beyond any system. The real seeker after Truth must be capable of penetrating into the essence of the meaning of all the different systems and synthesizing them into one-ness. Only then will the aspirant come close to the first degree of transformation in the

Great Work.

We cannot "distill" the meaning of the different kinds of Teachings and synthesize them by means of ordinary logical thinking or analogous deduction, but rather by *diving deep into the meaning beyond words*, by feeling with our awakening intuition, as it were, the inner meaning of every word and sentence. Only thus can an aspirant come to the final synthesis. It is not surprising that only knowledge or information is insufficient because it pertains only to one Center – the Intellect – and according to the Great Work we have five Centers, all of which have to be balanced so that the awakening of Essence/Soul is made possible. These five Centers are as follows:

1) The Instinctive Center, relating to the instinctive function of our bodies and the five senses.

2) The Movement Center, relating to the movement functions of our bodies, including the mechanical movements that take place in our minds (e.g. how we often will repeat a song or phrase over and over again in our mind).

3) The Emotional Center that relates to the feelings/emotions. In this important Center are located all the great forces in a human being. Through great love in her heart, a tiny little nurse, Florence Nightingale, was able to help many suffering soldiers during the Crimean war and become a great name in history. Through the power of compassion, Henry Dunant built up the Red Cross which has lasted until the present day and benefited all humanity, especially during times of famine and war. It is through the power of love stemming from the Emotional Center, and not through a great intellect, that these prodigious acts are accomplished.

4) The Intellectual Center has the function of gathering information, collecting, analyzing, comparing, organizing and synthesizing data. Hence to approach the Great Work

with just this one Center will not lead the student too far.

5) The Sex Center is also very important as within it is located the heart of the ordinary human being. Witness the way an elderly woman will still rouge her sunken cheeks and color her shriveled lips and listen to romantic songs, will still build up sweet "castles in the air", endlessly awaiting her prince charming who will never arrive, or the sweet beloved that will care for her in the future and give her all the joys and comforts she has been longing for. This *hope* for the beloved, for happiness, for the beautiful romance is what keeps the heart of ordinary humanity alive. An aspirant in the Great Work, however, must be aware of this energy which is located in the Sex Center and channel it consciously and with all his/her effort into the search for Greater Knowledge – a knowledge that is very different than the common "knowledge" we need for our ordinary mundane existence, e.g., how to make money, how to be successful in our jobs, how to achieve an honorable position in society etc. It is only by the use of this energy of the Sex Center which is usually wasted through day-dreaming, building castles in the air, living on false hopes that will never come etc., that we can transform ourselves. By directing this energy to a higher level we can penetrate into the deeper Truth, obtain Esoteric Knowledge and come closer to the Mystery of the Great Work.

Therefore the Great Work has to be approached with all the five Centers. All the energies that are leaked out and scattered through the Centers have to be collected into one-pointedness and this energy has to be used for *inner concentration* to observe scientifically our five Centers. Thus may we fulfill the oracle of Delphi, "Man know Thyself" – and only then are we ready to study the Science of Transformation.

Knowledge of the above science is needed to transform one

being into another of a higher order. It is similar to the energy needed for the caterpillar to transform itself into a butterfly. Transformation does not happen in an instant, it is a slow, preparatory process that takes place over a long and gradual period of time. In order for the caterpillar to become the butterfly it first must go through the stage of the chrysalis. It has to give up all the activities of the caterpillar, withdraw all its energy inwards and be silent. Then in silence, the energy needed for transformation will proceed to do its work, until finally, the caterpillar will emerge as the lively butterfly.

Generally people do not see the whole underlying process of transformation but are only aware of its dramatic moment – the point at which the chrysalis becomes the butterfly. Many Zen stories illustrate this dramatic moment of transformation without mentioning the painstaking process in the stage of the chrysalis which entails rigorous, day-by-day discipline for many years in the eradication of the personality in order to achieve this metamorphosis.

Transformation can be accomplished in two ways. One is by faith and *obedience to the instructions of a real and good Teacher*, performing the discipline meticulously day by day for many years. The other way is by following the Path of Knowledge which is more suitable to this Aquarian Age. In this latter case transformation must be done consciously by using our intelligence and awareness to observe the totality of our mind/ Chitta, by controlling and organizing the modifications or *vrittis* of our Chitta in an ordered, 7th Ray way. By following this method we can achieve transformation gradually, scientifically and efficiently.

Indeed, the science of transformation in the Great Work is based on scientific, hidden laws. It is similar to charging up an electrical generator, escalating the energy from lower to higher voltage until finally a tremendous power is produced, controlled by our awakened Central Awareness and "anchored" in the Law of Love and Wisdom. Only when the aspirant has arrived at this point can he experience the *dramatic climax of the Great Awakening or the birth of his Soul on its own plane.*

The key point in mastering the *vrittis* of the mind/Chitta is *Ahamkara*, the "I-maker". It is a faculty within our being which continuously creates the feeling of "I" and the changes according to different situations or surroundings: it is that faculty within us that creates all our varied multiplicity of thoughts and emotions. We have to watch our whole being carefully with regard to this *Ahamkara* or "I-maker", because through it we can lose our energy or Shakti. Through this *Ahamkara*, which creates the many groups of "I"s within our psyche, our being and consequently our Karma is determined. A person who has a good life, while another person who consists of many conflicting groups of "I"s is confused and difficult and his life of contradictory events.

Hence, first of all, we have to look into and arrange the different group of "I"s within us in a harmonious way. These different group of "I"s are like vortices within our Chitta around which gather thoughts and emotions which repeat themselves mechanically over and over again. These collective groups of "I"s with their repetitive thoughts and emotions are from what is called our personality, our conditioning. Hence a person is conditioned by his tradition, his education, the country in which he is born and raised, his religion, the food he eats etc. We can, therefore, make the conclusion that an ordinary man consists of nothing more than a group of *Ahamkara* with their repetitive thoughts and emotions (impressions or *vasanas* and *samskaras*). In a certain sense, an ordinary man is nothing more than a bundle of vasanas or vrittis that repeat themselves over and over again: intellectually with his own opinions and prejudices, emotionally with his own likes and dislikes, sexually with his ideal types of beauty, instinctively with his own particular taste preferences, and a Movement Center with its various activities in sports or crafts. But as a man decides to take upon himself the task of the Great Work, he has no other alternative than to awaken and separate himself from his conditioning *vasanas* and *vrittis* of all his Centers.

Besides his body and the five Centers that form his personality, man consists of something more, even though it is latent. This is what we call the Essence or Soul in incarnation. Some of the characteristics of the **Essence** are naturalness, originality, the love of Truth, compassion, devotion, discrimination between the false and the real; while the characteristics of personality are mechanicality, rigidity, coldness, imitation, indifference to the feelings of others, arrogance, defensiveness, self-importance, self-centeredness, self-love (which when it turns negative manifest as self-pity, depression, continuous complaints, destructive criticism, aggression, self-destruction etc.).

In fact, personality is nothing more than a hardened, crystallized group of "I"s that is created through a projected self-image of what we want to be and the desire to be regarded by the world as such. But *Essence* is our true individuality, our own being as we really are – not as the environment wants us to be. When a person is bored by living artificially, according to his imaginary "I" which forms his false personality, by the dictates of his environment or the society in which he lives, then he begins to search for what is true and real. At first he will accomplish this search by absorbing the many truths that are available through reading spiritual books or listening to genuine teachers. These truths will gradually set him free from the illusion of the life of his personality and lift him up to be his real "self".

But this process of awakening is not at all easy and simple, because as the man is trying to awaken in his Essence, many forces within him will resist and hinder his purpose. An average aspirant is not capable of staying awake continuously all day. He can be awake for a few minutes, a few hours...but then he goes to sleep again, carried away by his ordinary mechanical group of "I"s and his many petty habits. Only when he is again pondering on the ideas of the Great Work, the group of "I"s that loves the Work will be reactivated and will lift him up on a higher level of consciousness. In these few moments of awakening, he must use his discrimination to observe himself and gradually discover the Science of Transformation. Through this process of self-observation, he will see the many groups of "I"s within him.

These groups of "I"s can be categorized into five divisions:

1) The Big Group of "I"s that form the majority of his being, the core of his ordinary human self and with which he makes important decisions and determines the course of his life.

2) The petty group of "I"s that form his little peculiarities – whether he likes to wear black shoes instead of brown, or his preference is for a grilled cheese or roast beef sandwich etc.

3) The Work group of "I"s that is interested in the mysteries of Life and Death, the noumenon behind ephemeral events, the enigma of Time, Eternity and so on. This group of "I"s is, of course, very important and has to be cultivated.

4) A group of "I"s that are negative or antagonistic to the Work, that will sabotage every step and hinder the progress of the aspirant. This group of "I"s has to be scrutinized seriously and observed continuously and ultimately they have to be thoroughly eliminated.

5) A neutral group of "I"s that in itself is harmless but that has to be watched, as some of them may form a link or bridge to the negative group of "I"s which are against the Work.

From the practical view point of the Work, we can divide these groups of "I"s into three:

1) The group of "I"s that love the Work and are determined

to tread the Path.

2) The group of "I"s that are antagonistic to the Work. These have to be gradually but definitely eliminated, otherwise we will never be able to crystallize our Essence and become an awakened Soul.

3) The neutral group of "I"s that relates our being to our mundane life in the world: our profession, our duties to family, society etc. But again, we have to watch this group of "I"s carefully because around some of them a connection could be made with the antagonistic, destructive group of "I"s which will drag us down to a negative, melancholy state and discourage us from performing the tasks of the Great Work. This neutral group of **"I"s** have to be put under the continuous control of our awakening Essence which is strengthened by the Work group **"I"s**.

Further, we have to take heed of the existence of all these groups of "I"s that are oriented towards the Work from the lower energy level into a higher energy level. Of course, first we have to understand the Work ideas correctly. Then, as we penetrate deeply into the meaning of every Work idea for a long time, we build up a "Work *vritti*" and *samskara* within our mind. This "Work *samskara*" becomes, as it were, a ladder of Light and a pole of Peace which we can hold on to in times of confusion and conflict when the antagonistic group of "I"s are fighting us and trying to pull us down into the habits and desires of our ordinary mechanical life. We must be able to hold on to this "ladder of Light" and "pole of Peace" until we are surrounded and enclosed with vibrant and powerful living ideas of the Great Work. These ideas must be built up like a strong, huge building made of solid concrete within which we can take our refuge and protection when the conditions of life become difficult or unbearable. Only then have we found the way to true Peace and developed real Faith.

But after all, this is only the first step. After crystallizing all the ideas of the Work, we become more stable and become Man #4. Now we approach life in a different way – from the point of view of the Work and so, according to one of the great hidden Laws: "Your being attracts your Life", the Karma of our life will change because now our being, our attitude and our way of thinking has changed. We will no longer be struggling and toiling and working hard for the sake of our ordinary job or our many little desires or even for survival. The Divine Laws will protect and shelter us as we have raised our being up from the mundane level of the Lunar pitris. Law of Karma will open further possibilities for us as we tread the Path of Light.

The next step – after this structure of the ideas of the Work has been built firmly within our Chitta – is to penetrate these ideas of the Work in the higher dimensions. As we know, related to the Ray of Creation and man's position in the Universe, the five Centers are made of the substance of the Lunar pitris while the Essence or Soul and higher faculties of man are created from the substance and forces of the sun. So even though we have acquired knowledge of the Work ideas, it is still not sufficient to transform our being because our Centers themselves still consist of the substance of the Lunar pitris which have their own desires and the continuous tendency to feed the Lunar Lords. Hence, after accumulating the necessary Work ideas, we still have to acquire knowledge of the Science of Transformation in order to crystallize the Work group of "I"s into Essence and also transform the matter of our five Centers, consisting of the Lunar pitris, into Solar substance.

This can only be accomplished by invoking Solar Powers from the higher dimensions; it cannot be done merely with our own force. According to Esoteric Tradition it is said that we have to open our hearts to the higher Energies of the Great Work. We have to open our heart and make it receptive, like a chalice or a lotus, to receive this Divine Energy from Solar origin. Then this Divine Solar Energy which is like an elixir will slowly and gradually penetrate and transmute the substance of our being into the level of the frequency of the Sun. Esoteric Tradition mentions that this invocation of Solar Energy can be done by chanting the Mantra of Avlokiteshvare, Who is the Manifested Divine Logos, emanating from the "heart of the Spiritual Sun". This Divine Shakti is like a golden tongue of Flame shooting out from the Divine Flame of the Solar Logos, and as the chanting of the Mantra takes place, it flows down to all the Centers and gradually transmutes the Lunar substance into Solar Energy.

Of course there will be hindrances – our Centers will rebel tremendously because they have to undergo death and transformation and therefore do not want to surrender. But this is our task and all depends on our one-pointedness and dedication to be constantly aligned with the downpouring Solar Energy in the process of chanting the Mantra.

Always keep in mind that the chanting of the Mantra has to be strictly done in a state of self-remembering because only in that state will the Solar Energy flow down to our Essence and gradually eliminate and transform all the Lunar forces within our being. To chant the Mantra correctly, we have to open our hearts and attune our Chitta with Its Divine Rhythm. By vibrating our Chitta to this Divine Rhythm for a long time, the substance of our Chitta and the substance of our five Centers will be "soaked" and filled with the Divine Energy of the Mantra of Avalokiteshvara. As this process takes place the Energy continues to flow down to our Pranamaya kosha or Etheric body and also penetrates our Prana. Further, it continues to have an effect on our physical body or Anamaya kosha, and on our metabolism via the Chakras and endocrine glands.

It is at this point that a life of physical purity is necessary and we have to be very careful that the food we eat consists only of *sattvic* elements, for if it consists of *rajasic* or *tamasic* elements, then this low level energy of our body will clash with the higher

215

Solar Energy coming down from our Chitta via our etheric body with the result that we could develop many diseases. Hence the body should be kept in a yen state and the food intake through our Anamaya kosha has to be chosen from *sattvic* elements. Only then, when our whole Chitta and all our five Centers and Pranamaya kosha are filled with Solar Energy, is the aspiring disciple ready to accomplish the Great Awakening and transform himself into Man#5. It is at this point that the aspirant becomes a crystallized living Soul and enters the Inner Circle of humanity (Hierarchy).

**** OM MANI PADME HUM ****

Notes

(1) Pg. 71, *One Hundred Thousand Songs of Milarepa*, Garma C.C. Chang, Oriental Studies Foundation, USA.

(2) IBID pg. 80

(3) Pg. 210, *The Rays and the Initiations*, Alice A.Bailey, Lucis Publishing Company, New York.

(4) Pg. 79, *One Hundred Thousand Songs of Milarepa*, Garma C.C. Chang, Oriental Studies Foundation, USA.

(5) Pg. 73 *Treatise on White Magic*, Alice. A.Bailey, Lucis Publishing Co. N.Y.

(6) Pg. 210, *One Hundred Thousand Songs of Milarepa*, Garma C.C. Chang

(7) Pg. 12, *The Voice of the Silence and other chosen Fragments*, H.P.Blavatsky, The Theosophy Company, Los Angeles

(8) Pg 920. *A Treatise on Cosmic Fire*, Alice.A.Bailey, Lucis Publishing Company, New York

(9) Pg. 52, *Our Glorious Future*, Mabel Collins, Theosophical Book Shop, Edinburgh

(10) Pg.926, *Treatise on Cosmic Fire*, footnote Mantric Sounds, Alice. A.Bailey, Lucis Publishing Co. N.Y.

(11) Pg. 6-7, *Voice of the Silence*, H.P.Blavatsky. The Theosophy Company, LA

(12) Pg. 198, *Discipleship in the New Age*, Alice. A.Bailey, Lucis Publishing Co. N.Y.

(13) Pg. 4, *Light on the Path*, Mabel Collins, Theosophical University Press, California.

(14) Pg. 207 *Esoteric Astrology*, Alice. A.Bailey, Lucis Publishing Co. N.Y.

(15) Pg. 184 *A Treatise on White Magic*, Alice A. Bailey, Lucis Publishing Company, New York

(16) Pg.25 *Voice of the Silence*, H.P.Blavatsky, The Theosophy Company, LA

(17) Pg. 17 *Voice of the Silence*

(18) Pg. 692-3, *Esoteric Psychology, Volume 2*, Alice. A.Bailey, Lucis Publishing Co. NY

(19) Pg. 688-89 *IBID*

(20) Pg.629, *Discipleship in the New Age, Vol.1*, Alice. A.Bailey, Lucis Publishing Co.

(21) Pg. 699, *Esoteric Psychology, Vol.2*, Alice. A.Bailey, Lucis Publishing Co. N.Y.

(22) Pg. 1, *Blog New Jersey Metaphysical Society*, by author

(23) Pg. 27, *Labours of Hercules*, Alice. A.Bailey, Lucis Publishing Co. N.Y.

(24) Pg. 595, *A Treatise on Cosmic Fire...*

(25) Pg. 4, *Light on the Path...*

(26) Pg. 13 *Voice of the Silence*

(27) Pg. 86 *Rays and Initiation*

(28) Pg. 578 *IBID*

(29) Pg. 191 *IBID*

(30) Pg. 85 *Secret talks with Mr. G.*,IDHHB, INC. 1978

(31) Pg. 86 *IBID*

(32) Pg.13 *Voice of the Silence*, H.P.B.

(33) Pg.71 *One Hundred Thousand Songs of Milarepa*

(34) Pg. 338 *The Mahatma Letters*, A.P. Sinnett, Theosophical Publishing House, Adyar

(35) Pg.77 *One Hundred Thousand Songs of Milasrepa*,

Bibliography

Challoner, H.K. *The Wheel of Rebirth* (London: Theosophical Publishing House)

Collins, Mabel. *Blossom and the Fruit* (California: Health Research, (1890))

Gamow, George. *123 Infinity* (New York: Dover Publications INC)

Lytton, Bulwer. *Zanoni* (New York, USA: Rudolf Steiner Publication)

Raja Yoga, Swami *Ramacharaka* (Chicago: Yogi Publication Society 1906)

Taimini, I.K. *The Science of Yoga*, (Wheaton, USA Theosophical Publishing House)

AXIS MUNDI
BOOKS

Axis Mundi Books
EXPLORING THE WORLD OF HIDDEN KNOWLEDGE

Axis Mundi Books provide the most revealing and coherent explorations and investigations of the world of hidden or forbidden knowledge. Take a fascinating journey into the realm of Esoteric Mysteries, High Magic (non-pagan), Mysticism, Mystical Worlds, Goddess, Angels, Aliens, Archetypes, Cosmology, Alchemy, Gnosticism, Theosophy, Kabbalah, Secret Societies and Religions, Symbolism, Quantum Theory, Conspiracy Theories, Apocalyptic Mythology, Unexplained Phenomena, Holy Grail and Alternative Views of Mainstream Religion.

If you have enjoyed this book, why not tell other readers by posting a review on your preferred book site?

Recent bestsellers from Axis Mundi Books are:

On Dragonfly Wings
A Skeptic's Journey to Mediumship
Daniela I. Norris
Daniela Norris, former diplomat and atheist, discovers
communication with the other side following the sudden death
of her younger brother.
Paperback: 978-1-78279-512-4 ebook: 978-1-78279-511-7

Inner Light
The Self-Realization via the Western Esoteric Tradition
P.T. Mistlberger
A comprehensive course in spiritual development using the
powerful teachings of the Western esoteric tradition.
Paperback: 978-1-84694-610-3 ebook: 978-1-78279-625-1

The Seeker's Guide to Harry Potter
Dr Geo Trevarthen
An in-depth analysis of the mythological symbols and themes
encountered in the Harry Potter series, revealing layers of
meaning beneath the surface of J K Rowling's stories.
Paperback: 978-1-84694-093-4 ebook: 978-1-84694-649-3

The 7 Mysteries
Your Journey from Matter to Spirit
Grahame Martin
By simply reading this book you embark on a journey of
transformation from the world of matter into spirit.
Paperback: 978-1-84694-364-5

Angel Healing & Alchemy
How To Begin Melchisadec, Sacred Seven & the Violet Ray
Angela McGerr
Angelic Healing for physical and spiritual harmony.
Paperback: 978-1-78279-742-5 ebook: 978-1-78279-337-3

Colin Wilson's 'Occult Trilogy'
A Guide for Students
Colin Stanley
An essential guide to Colin Wilson's major writings on the
occult.
Paperback: 978-1-84694-706-3 ebook: 978-1-84694-679-0

The Heart of the Hereafter
Love Stories from the End of Life
Marcia Brennan
This book can change not only how we view the end of life,
but how we view life itself and the many types of love we
experience.
Paperback: 978-1-78279-528-5 ebook: 978-1-78279-527-8

Kabbalah Made Easy
Maggy Whitehouse
A down to earth, no-red-strings-attached look at the mystical
tradition made famous by the Kabbalah Center.
Paperback: 978-1-84694-544-1 ebook: 978-1-84694-890-9

The Whole Elephant Revealed
Insights Into the Existence and Operation of Universal Laws
and the Golden Ratio
Marja de Vries
An exploration of the universal laws which make up the
dynamic harmony and balance of the universe.
Paperback: 978-1-78099-042-2 ebook: 978-1-78099-043-9

Readers of ebooks can buy or view any of these bestsellers by clicking on the live link in the title. Most titles are published in paperback and as an ebook. Paperbacks are available in traditional bookshops. Both print and ebook formats are available online.
Find more titles and sign up to our readers' newsletter at http://www.johnhuntpublishing.com/mind-body-spirit
Follow us on Facebook at https://www.facebook.com/OBooks
and Twitter at https://twitter.com/obooks